INTERCEPTORS

INTERCEPTORS:

THE UNTOLD FIGHT AGAINST THE MEXICAN CARTELS

MATTHEW THOMAS

INTERCEPTORS
The Untold Fight Against the Mexican Cartels

Cover Design by Joe Verbanac, owner of J&C Design and Marketing, and Joey Nobody, owner of Artistic Development Group LLC.

Editing by DragonflyWings.Ink
a division of Lori Lynn Enterprises LLC

Internal Formatting by Meg Delagrange

Published in the United States of America.

WARNINGS

INTENSE GRAPHIC VIOLENCE, strong language, profanity, and frightening images are used to describe the author's experiences with the Mexican drug cartels. As such, the content of this book is not suitable for children. The language used to describe experiences with the Mexican drug cartel may be offensive to sensitive readers. Please exercise caution while reading, listening to, or recommending this book.

DISCLAIMERS

THE FOLLOWING VIEWPOINTS and accounts in this book are those of Matthew Thomas, who has worked for the Pinal County Sheriff's Office in several different assignments spanning approximately three decades.

The intention of this book is to share his story about growing up immersed in the Mexican culture and gang-infested neighborhoods, the things he has learned, and what has worked for him throughout his life and law enforcement journey.

These views and accounts are based on personal experiences from his life and his law enforcement and leadership careers.

All attempts have been made to verify the information provided by this publication. Neither the author nor the publisher assumes any responsibility for errors, omissions, or contrary interpretations of the subject matter herein.

This book is for information and entertainment purposes only. The views expressed are those of the author alone and should not be taken as expert instruction or commands. The reader is responsible for his or her future actions.

Neither the author nor the publisher assumes any responsibility or liability on the behalf of the purchaser or reader of these materials.

CONTENTS

This book is dedicated to the men and women who have chosen to enter the arena as law enforcement officers and their everyday battles to fight for good and suppress the ever-present evil. I salute you, your endless sacrifices, and the sacrifices of your families and loved ones. It is you, the fine men and women who hold that thin blue line. You, my friends, are the difference between order and chaos. Keep pushing forward, because yours is a higher calling, and the world cannot survive without you.

FOREWORD

THE DESERTS OF ARIZONA are dry and harsh. With the reputation of the Wild West still ringing true, it's a place that requires tested, righteous, and strong men to run to calls of danger.

The Pinal County Sheriff's Office knows this well, and Matthew Thomas has been running to those calls for nearly thirty years.

Born and raised in South Phoenix, Thomas was no stranger to the bad guys. The streets in the Valley of the Sun made him tough and taught "the gringo" about the fragility of the thin blue line. I've known this man for a decade and have been privileged to watch him work both from afar and up close.

In 2011, Lieutenant Thomas took me as a hungry young journalist on my first ride-along through the desert. I met him in a parking lot in Casa Grande and hopped into the front seat of his dusty unmarked SUV. As a member of the SWAT team, he dressed the part in a dark green tactical uniform and gear. There, in his "office," he taught me the harsh realities of child exploitation, trafficking, drug running, and the danger that lurks in the dark corners of society. I learned about the border battle against the cartels, who engage in pure violence without regret. I saw up close the havoc they wreak on American communities and the environment.

The cities near the intersection where we started, which used to be predominantly ranching and farming communities, are Casa Grande, Arizona City, Maricopa, Hidden Valley, Eloy, and Stanfield. Although some farms still exist, this area is inundated with cartel activity. The bad guys, members of the Sinaloa cartel, live there, run stash houses, and have turned access roads, right next to farms that have been in operation for decades, into major smuggling routes.

While we drove, we were closely watched through the binocular glasses of armed cartel spotters in the mountains that surrounded us. In Spanish, over their radios, they communicate with a network in the hilltops about how to best avoid detection. I looked to the back of the SUV and was comforted by a rifle loosely stored within arm's reach.

A decade later, after staying in regular touch, I went to visit again in April 2021. It was past time to learn some new lessons and be reminded of the old ones. This time, I met Chief Deputy Thomas at headquarters in Florence.

After checking in and being escorted through security, I took the elevator to another floor. When the doors opened, I walked down the hall and into his corner office, full of awards and years of documented memories. This time, as the Sheriff's Executive Officer and Chief Deputy, he had on a perfectly pressed dress uniform. He met me with a smile and shook my hand with a challenge coin.

After decades of work in every level of the department, completing and leading over 700 missions, Chief Deputy Thomas had been promoted. He was now in charge of overseeing operations for hundreds of employees and covering territory that encompasses 5,400 square miles and more than 450,000 people. Despite his promotion past everyone else, paying all of his dues along the way, he spent the day personally taking me back to the desert.

Kicking off the morning, we sped down dirt roads and the highway to catch up with a high-speed chase.

Upon our arrival, other law enforcement was on the scene making an arrest. Thomas took the opportunity to put on his Kevlar vest and made sure his carbine rifle was readily available for the next location. There, we could encounter active human smuggling, and the people in charge wouldn't be happy to see us. Bodies are a lucrative product, and thousands of people are being moved across the desert by ruthless criminal organizations.

As he showed me fresh remnants of a smuggling scene, he carefully and calmly surveyed the surroundings with his long gun in tow. A quiet danger was close. Tension was in the air.

Back at the office, we said goodbye, and I said a prayer. May God protect the heroes who work to keep the wolves at bay.

Chief Deputy Matthew Thomas has one hell of a story to tell about his life and work. Lucky for us, he's taking us along for the ride.

—Katie Pavlich

INTRODUCTION

ALL COPS IN THE WORLD have a collection of stories in their heads from the calls they have been on and operations they have participated in. These cops have also had the opportunity to tell these stories while hanging out with friends and family around a table or a campfire.

The stories focus on the calls or the wild things they have seen when doing the job. Quite frankly, as cops, most of us view these as just ordinary stories that go along with the job. But I can tell you—from doing this work for over twenty-eight years now—that truth is very often stranger than fiction.

Some of the calls and stories are so wild and crazy that you would have to be either a genius or a madman to make them up. I have now spent almost three decades doing this type of work in various capacities.

My assignments have included working in Detention, Patrol, Traffic, Training, SWAT, and Narcotics. I have worked my way through the ranks, holding positions as a Deputy, SWAT Operator, Detective, Sergeant, SWAT Team Leader, Lieutenant and SWAT Commander, and now in my current assignment as the Sheriff's Executive Officer.

Now that I have moved into a more administrative role, I have had more opportunities to tell stories from the "good ol' days." I am not as hesitant as I once was to talk about some of the great work I had the honor of being a part of.

While telling one of these stories one day, a good friend said that this unbelievable stuff needed to be in a book. I just laughed it off at the time. I mean, come on, I don't know the first thing about writing a book. Hell, I wouldn't even know how to start, and even if I did, who would be interested enough or care enough to read it?

These were all just experiences that I considered to be some of the best parts of doing this job, some of the great times I had in this career, and some of the cool shit I have had the honor of doing.

Nonetheless, the seed had been planted even though I had self-doubt and apprehension about even trying. This was just my career, and while I have had some fun doing it, I doubted that my stories could be book-worthy. But now, there was this nagging, lingering thought of *why not?*

I explored this thought a little further and began scrolling through my memories of the many operations and crazy things I had been a part of. In doing this, I realized that these were not just stories. Through them, I was actually the carrier of our history. These stories keep that history alive and honor the men and women who took part in them.

I also want people to understand what took place on a day-to-day basis, especially as it related to our fight against the cartels in our county and our state. Putting these stories on paper would help accomplish that. We were in one hell of a fight against the bad guys, and it continues to this day.

So, I chose to bite the bullet and just do it. I decided to start writing and documenting what I had seen and been through during these operations. I want to take you from the early part of my career through today to show you what we faced and how we dealt with each problem. My hope is that this gives you an inside view into our fight, looking through the eyes of a guy who was right in the mix of it.

As I take you through some of the operations I was involved in—specifically, those conducted in the open desert areas—you should understand that they were unique. Only a tiny percentage of U.S. law enforcement has had the privilege of working in such operations.

When we first began conducting "desert ops," we simply applied law enforcement tactics to large, open areas. But through trial and error, we quickly found that these operations required military tactics. We were essentially conducting military-type patrols; we had to worry about things like high points, overlooks, and ambushes. So we developed our tactics, techniques, and procedures (TTPs) to conduct these operations. We then constantly made adjustments based on our successes and failures. Again, there was no model to follow. We created the model as we went along.

I want to cut through all of the political bullshit and give you a true, ground-level view of the fight against evil along the southwest border of Arizona. Our fight has been going on for years. But recently, the border activity gained quite a bit of popularity in the media—mainly because

Mexican cartels and illegal immigration have become very hot political topics in our country. This, in turn, has brought to light the fight we had been waging for years and also highlighted the work going on behind the scenes.

Quite frankly, most people, even those who live and work in this state, have no idea what was—and still is—happening right in front of them. The time period I'm talking about is now referred to as "those Wild West days" by many of us who worked then, as it was pretty damn unique and dangerous. I hope to give you a little peek into the craziness and tell you about some of the unreal things that went on behind the curtain of camouflage that cloaks the hidden world of crime from the everyday world.

As I take you through this journey, I will provide background on the cartels from historical data and my firsthand experience and knowledge. I will describe the culture of the cartels and how it is intertwined with Mexican culture. I will introduce you to the cops behind the operations that target these cartels. Ultimately, I'll give you a front row seat to the very unique world of fighting huge, criminal organizations.

I will also give you as much background and context as possible because there are always stories within these stories. The more information and groundwork I can lay out for you, the better understanding you will have of how it looked and felt to be in the middle of it and why we did things the way we did.

You will need to remember that all of this is from the perspective of a mere county cop lacking the resources of the larger federal agencies. My hope is that you will gain an appreciation for the fact that this is not something we can defeat without every willing and able person standing with us in the fight. It takes a community to suppress and defeat the evil of the criminals behind these cartels. It takes parents, students, brothers, and sisters coming together with community leaders and law enforcement to stand firmly against evil.

The cartels are not just a problem in the U.S. They have branched out worldwide and have also decimated their own country. They have turned the great, historic, beautiful country that is Mexico into an all-out war zone. These cartels have transformed the newer generations of young Mexican people into people who do not value human life, idolize wealth and the fast life, and do not hold onto their beautiful Mexican heritage.

More than anything, I want you to see and feel the daily heroic battles involving our heroes in law enforcement—from the local deputies and city police, to our state's brothers and sisters, to our many federal partners. It is a coordinated effort by all of us in law enforcement to fight these bastards.

Having worked in law enforcement since the early 1990s, I have watched the game change over the years. I have also had the opportunity to watch the cartels grow into what they are today. I have had a front-row seat to the greatest show on earth and have been involved in the good-versus-evil battle for over a quarter of a century. I have had the distinct honor and privilege of working with some of the most extraordinary people in the world in our law enforcement community.

While we are at a place in our history where our profession is under scrutiny, and new accusations fly almost daily on local and social media, I can tell you this: I am part of a profession that was built on honor and integrity. The people who do this job, often thanklessly, have sworn an oath before their God to perform their duties and protect those who cannot defend themselves against evil—evil that many people refuse to acknowledge even exists.

My last hope in sharing these stories is that you will gain a true understanding of the individual people behind the badge, who choose to work in this crazy profession of law enforcement. They put their lives on the line for their communities and subject themselves and their families to some pretty awful and dangerous stuff as part of their everyday jobs.

Some housekeeping notes: I have changed a few names to protect the privacy of those involved who prefer to stay off the proverbial radar. The specific tactics, techniques, and equipment I discuss will not negatively affect operational security today because they are no longer considered trade secrets. They are either old, outdated, or open-source information that makes them no longer protected. I am keeping other details ambiguous to safeguard equipment, tactics, techniques, or methods that are still relevant. Essentially, the goal is to give you the best picture possible without compromising current operations.

Additionally, these are my memories based on my best recollection of events that took place over approximately a decade. In some cases, I have also talked to former teammates and partners to get their recollections of these same events. These stories are a result of all these memories and discussions.

When you read this book and these stories, I want to ensure that you understand some of the semantics. You will often hear me refer to co-workers as "guys" or "boys," and there are a couple of reasons for this.

First and foremost, it is just a habit to use general terms such as guys when referring to our fellow officers and sometimes even suspects. For example, I may say, "Those guys were some of the best I worked with." In this case, "guys" is commonly used to describe both men and women among my counterparts.

Another reason for these semantics is that the world of policing is, in fact, a male-dominated profession. When you look at policing as a whole, there is a much higher percentage of male police officers than female ones. I'm not saying this is good or bad; it is just a fact. I can say with certainty that the females in this profession are every bit as good at being cops as their male counterparts. In fact—and I often say this when I teach about undercover work—I feel strongly that a good female undercover officer will outper-form her male counterpart in that role most of the time.

I just want to make sure that you, as the reader, under-stand where I am coming from, and I understand that what I say and how I say it matters to people. My general use of these terms should in no way suggest that I value one over the other.

To help you get a bird's-eye view of the world of fight-ing the Mexican cartels, first I'll need to paint a picture of the terrain.

PINAL COUNTY: THE PERFECT SETTING FOR A DRUG WAR

Arizona has always held smuggling routes from Mexico into the United States, with some of these routes going back to the days of Pancho Villa in the late 1800s. They have been used and exploited by criminal elements on both sides of the border for over one hundred years.

These days, there are ports of entry between the U.S. and Mexico. In Arizona, we have six ports at the international border with Mexico. The ports that most directly affect our county are Nogales and Lukeville. Between these two ports lie hundreds of miles of open and minimally populated desert, and the international border is nothing more than a three-strand barbed-wire fence in some locations.

In other locations, there is an actual border fence or barrier, which does, in fact, prohibit the majority of illegal crossings. That makes the crossing areas that lead to Pinal County even more attractive and effectively pushes the traffickers directly into Pinal County.

Add to that the fact that much of this area also sits on the Tohono O'Odham Indian Reservation—a sovereign nation within the United States that also crosses into Mexico. With minimal interference, the cartels can transport their product across the border and into the U.S. So, they exert a high level of control over this area and regularly use it with impunity.

The open desert between the two ports of entry has minimal population and law enforcement. The terrain in this area consists of high desert mountains that start at the border and run approximately seventy miles north into Pinal County and right up to Interstate 8.

The mountain ranges curve and somewhat diverge at the northern end to create the effect of a funnel right into the southwest corner of our county. The mountains also have large valleys between them consisting of wide-open desert with small Indian villages or towns spread throughout. There is a network of paved roads, dirt roads, and four-wheel-drive roads webbed throughout this area.

These details equal very attractive terrain to the cartels as they can watch from the mountains over the valleys. The cartels can implant their members into the Indian villages. They can control the routes that run from the border to the first real civilization, which is Pinal County in the area of Interstate 8.

Interstate 8 then becomes the new goal line. Once the cartels reach Interstate 8 and the surrounding small communities of Stanfield, Maricopa, and Casa Grande, they can temporarily store their product in local houses that they own.

These houses are commonly referred to as "stash houses" and look no different from other houses in that area. But drugs, weapons, money, and people are stored there. Once the product hits these stash houses, it can stay there for a while or immediately get transferred to different vehicles to be transported to the Phoenix area for further distribution.

The interstate is usually where the cartels load people transporting drugs by foot (called "packers") into vehicles. It is also where the people who crossed the border illegally and are heading further into the U.S. get picked up and taken to a stash house.

Sometimes the cartels will opt to transport drugs or people straight into the Phoenix Metro area rather than use the local stash houses, and they do so using the interstate systems that run from this area into Phoenix.

A few rural routes wind across the reservations and the open desert north and into our county. As you get close to and into our county, these rural routes become better roads that lead straight to major roadways or interstates. It's easy for the cartels to use these roads, routes, and trails to move their people and products.

Then there is the steady supply of people willing to work with the cartels. I had always been aware of the illicit drug use and drug trade around me, but I did not realize that I was actually in the eye of the storm for cartel activity. My state, city, and even my neighborhood were the epicenter for street and prison gangs. The gangs worked hand in hand with each other to further the cartels that were at the top of this food chain.

And now you know why Pinal County, Arizona, was front and center in the drug war. If a movie producer had been looking for the perfect setting for a film about the Mexican drug cartel, Pinal County would have been at the top of the list. Envision the winding mountain ranges, the stash houses, and Interstate 8, and then imagine being a street cop trying to fight this war.

Operations that I describe throughout this book became the norm for quite some time, with chases, gunplay, and the ever-present danger of fighting the cartels taking place almost nightly in the wide-open deserts of our county. We didn't realize it then, but it was a historic time in law enforcement. What had become routine for us was actually some of the craziest cop work anyone had ever been involved in.

A cache of handheld radios and a vehicle-mounted radio used by
the cartels to communicate along the smuggling routes.

Signs in Pinal County smuggling corridors, which were placed on federal lands
under then-President Obama's administration

A group of backpackers in Pinal County, carrying what appears to be bulk marijuana packs. They are also
carrying water jugs to stay hydrated on the six-day walk from the U.S/Mexico border.

01.

FROM DESERT SUNRISE TO DEADLY GUNSHOTS

SHOTS FIRED! SHOTS FIRED!" exploded from the radio, shattering the early-morning silence. A massive rush of adrenaline immediately shot through my entire body. My heart pounded through my chest as I sat up in the driver's seat and made preparations to take off.

Where was I going? I had no idea, but I knew that I had to go. I was completely awake now, and the early-morning fog that hits you after an all-night shift was gone. My whole team had the same experience, and we were all bouncing from the adrenaline, waiting for the next radio transmission to piece together what was going on.

With its millions of beautiful stars shining as if God had tossed out diamonds across a black velvet bag, the dark desert night sky was becoming lighter as the sun approached the horizon. This time of morning had always been my favorite, as the sky silhouetting the eastern horizon mountains gradually lightened to blue. Splashes of pink and orange would mix in like a well-planned painting. This desert was beautiful, and I loved it. If only its beauty was not ruined by what I knew happened there daily.

It had been a long night with some activity, but honestly, we were all dead-ass tired from the multiday operation, and we were counting the minutes until we called it a night. Usually, this was when we would start winding down, begin stowing some of our gear from the overnight operation, and discuss a possible stop for breakfast before we hit the sack for the day.

I was with a few of the regular crew members on this particular night. We were running a desert interdiction operation. "Interdiction" means to disrupt, damage, destroy, capture, or cut off the cartel's ability to successfully operate within our country, state, and county. That was our job: to effectively insert ourselves as the line between the cartel's push from Mexico into the United States and our county.

A couple of media guys were embedded with us to capture these types of desert interdiction operations on camera. Usually, it was a curse when any media tagged along; we would get no activity and have no interdiction success. The past few nights had been different, though, and these guys were not typical media. Their work focused on telling positive stories about law enforcement, the military, and the work behind the scenes.

The producer was a former Air Force SERE (Survival, Evasion, Resistance, and Escape) Specialist, which translates to a badass who teaches special operations forces and other military personnel how to survive in the wild. While I didn't know him well at this point, my gut instinct told me that he was "one of my people." His cameraman seemed to be just as solid.

We were all wide awake and intently listening to the radio for clues as to where we needed to go. When the shots-fired transmission went across the radio, it was only natural that the radio channel exploded with activity.

We had several different agencies working together in this operation, with one main command post referred to as the TOC (Tactical Operations Center). The TOC was basically a police station on wheels. It would be parked within the operational area and used for briefings, storing equipment, processing, and debriefing. It was also a central point for communication and the recording point for the operation. All radio traffic requests, information output, and information recording would happen at the TOC.

All of a sudden, the radio channel sounded like a conference call with that awkward moment when everyone has something to say at the same time, but because there are no verbal cues to be seen, people begin interrupting and talking over one another in chaos. Now that we had an "event" taking place, all of the different units in the field flooded the TOC with radio traffic. Everyone had the same goal: figure out what was going on and who was taking fire.

The same "shots fired" voice came back again over the radio within minutes. He gave us their call sign, informing us that the gunfire did not hit them, and that the bad guy who shot at them had fled. As they shared this information, I could feel the adrenaline fueling my heart as the beats became more pronounced in my chest and neck. I was fully awake and started gathering up my gear.

Everyone in my vehicle grabbed their gear and prepared for what they knew would be a quick departure. There was no talking or coordinating. We all knew that there were good guys in trouble, and we were determined to get there and provide backup.

I stowed my M4 rifle next to me, securing it in a tight spot between my driver's seat and center console. This was not the spot made for a gun, but it worked great for quick deployment in situations like this. The stock fitted snugly, with the barrel pointed toward the floorboard next to the gas pedal. It stayed quite secure during aggressive driving maneuvers that were customary during these operations.

"I just need to know where you are," I mumbled to myself. "Come on, man … give us a location!" As if hearing my request, the voice came back with their location and possible direction the suspect was headed. Once we had that information to help our boys, and before they could finish their radio transmission, I smashed the skinny pedal on the right. With a little dirt thrown by my spinning tires, we were on the road.

Within minutes, we were rolling up to the location that everyone was converging on, a spot situated along Interstate 8. As we rolled up, we could see that everyone was good to go with no injuries. Once this was established, we obtained as much information as possible on the bad guys and the situation.

Our guys had encountered what they first thought was another law enforcement officer in the desert. He had some writing on his shirt that looked like the same "Police" or "Sheriff" raid shirts we often wear. It was only when this bad guy raised his weapon and fired a shot that they figured out, rather quickly, that this was not a fellow good guy.

But in a dynamic situation like this that takes place very rapidly, a lot of the details and follow-through become difficult. Our guys went into survival mode and scrambled for cover while preparing to return fire. The bad guy had the advantage, though, and he used this short time frame of confusion to escape. By the time the good guys had gained their senses again and realized they were no longer under fire, the bad guy had slipped away and had become a needle in a very large haystack.

We all set up in the area, trying to cover escape routes and find high ground to watch the desert valleys for any sign of the bad guy. Several teams began to backtrack to the location of the incident to look for clues and possibly track footprints.

We spent the next couple of hours saturating the area and following all leads that popped up, to no avail. Eventually, the reality set in that this guy had gotten away. The operation slowly began to break down as people were cleared to head home for the day.

There were plenty of nights when the bad guys all got away, and we were left to wonder how we ended up in these messes. I would often sit back and think about the fight we found ourselves in and wonder, *How is it that local county cops ended up running operations against one of the largest criminal syndicates in the world?*

But really the "how" didn't matter to me because when I looked back on these operations, I knew I was exactly where I was supposed to be ... where I was meant to be.

02.

INNER CITY
TRAINING GROUND

THE WORLD WE LIVE IN is truly cloaked in camouflage—much like the movie *The Matrix*, in which there is a dark, hidden world within the world we are aware of. Living in, working in, or even getting just a peek into the dark side of the world will show you things you honestly wish you could forget.

As a youngster growing up on the south side of what is now the fifth-largest city in the United States, I had a constant view of this dark side, where there was no shortage of criminals and drugs.

Looking back, I can't remember when I realized that I was living in a high-crime area, in a rough neighborhood called a "barrio." I don't remember a rampant and obvious drug problem either. There were just people who had gotten caught up in some type of criminal activity or used drugs. There were people you knew not to mess with, people we all joked about, and people we looked up to because of their status in the neighborhood.

I grew up in a predominantly Hispanic area, and I was the minority in my neighborhood. But while I was not Hispanic, being white did not prohibit me from their acceptance and a view into this culture.

Don't get me wrong, a non-Hispanic guy in a Hispanic neighborhood will get special names that identify him as such. Names like "Guero," a word used in Mexico to denote a person of fair complexion or blond hair, or "Gabacho," a Mexican term primarily used as a derogatory reference to an American. Being called these names was common for me, but it was cultural rather than hateful. Bottom line: my friends were my friends, and we all got along no matter our race. When you got down to it, we were all just kids living life and growing up like any other kids.

I was an only child with a mom who worked nights and slept during the day. Of course, because I grew up in a Hispanic neighborhood, I picked up certain Hispanic habits, mannerisms, and even a dialect.

Often, when I would go to family functions or parties at some of my friends' houses, I would gain the attention of some laughing adults while getting a plate of carne asada, beans, and rice, with a couple of tortillas. Then I would take my tortillas, ripping off small pieces, and use the small pieces like spoons to scoop up bites of my food. It doesn't seem extraordinary to anyone familiar with this, but it must have been odd for them to see a little white boy doing it.

I had learned this in elementary school when I stayed the night at my best friend's house. His mom was very traditional, and as we sat down to eat breakfast the next morning, she served us food, and I sat there waiting for my fork so I could tear into the chorizo with eggs. Finally, my friend asked why I wasn't eating, and I told him that I didn't have a fork to eat with. He and his brothers started laughing, and he said, "We don't use forks, pendejo." I looked at my plate, then looked at him and asked how I was supposed to eat. He showed me how to use a tortilla as an edible utensil.

This type of cultural education continued through my teenage years and even after high school as I began dating my future wife.

In the barrio, there was the neighborhood "newspaper"—the walls and fences that held the stories of the area. You could literally read the graffiti to see who was who, what was going on in the neighborhood, and where the gang boundaries were.

The boundaries are hard to explain because they were invisible lines drawn around blocks, neighborhoods, and gang territories. Sometimes you could be in the territory of one gang on one side of a road, and when you crossed the road, you landed in the territory of a different gang.

Growing up in this environment, you knew the boundaries well because your safety depended on them. I knew things like what neighborhoods I could walk in or through. In my teen years, I would often have to ride the city bus into central Phoenix with my friends. It would travel through several different territories, so we would have to know which bus stops were safe for us and which ones were not.

As I entered my first year of high school, I had to use the city bus to get to school and back, and it traveled from the south side of town into the central part of town. Because my mom worked into the evenings, I had to get off the bus on my way back home and spend a few hours at the local Chicanos Por La Causa doing my homework and playing basketball or pool.

The term "Chicano" refers to Mexican-Americans born in the United States, and it was popularized during the civil rights movement of the late 1960s. "Por La Causa" translates to "for the cause." Chicanos Por La Causa is a non-profit organization, and their building in the downtown area of Phoenix was open for kids to use.

The building was in a neighborhood that wasn't safe for me, so I had to make sure that I walked straight into the building as soon as I got off the bus. The building itself was somewhat of a green zone. Inside, it did not matter what neighborhood you were from, but everything was back in play once you left the building.

Whether in a gang or not, these were all the unspoken and unwritten rules that we had to follow. We were associated with whatever neighborhood we came from and who our friends were.

I remember the "gang cops" always rolling through our neighborhood in unmarked cars, stopping and talking to us. They would tell us all to sit on the sidewalk with our feet crossed, hands on our heads, while they searched us to ensure we didn't have any weapons.

We all carried knives at that time, mostly to cut oranges from the nearby orchards, but they would still give us a hard time about having them. They never confiscated them; they would just hold onto them while they suspiciously questioned us if the knives were really for oranges.

They would talk to us for a few minutes, mainly asking about any guys involved in the neighborhood gang or any neighborhood drama. Of course, the rules were that you never talked. If you did, you would be labeled a "snitch" and wouldn't be safe even in your own neighborhood. So we never talked about that stuff and gave the typical "I don't know anything" answers. The cops would then stand us up, give us our knives back, and be on their way.

In my elementary school days, we didn't think, *My friend's uncle is a real bad guy* or *My girlfriend's dad is a criminal.* We didn't look at these things the same way outsiders looking in did—they were just friends and the families of those friends. For me, these were just other kids that I went to school with, played sports with, and hung out with. Their families were just their families. I knew them as moms and dads, uncles or brothers.

It never really occurred to us that our friend's uncle with all of the tattoos who just got out of prison was a bad guy. As kids, we just saw that the guy who was gone for a long time was now back, and the family was happy to see him. He would talk about the fights he had been in or the other legendary guys from the neighborhood he had hung out with in prison. Or he'd tell stories from before getting "locked up."

As I got older, I figured out exactly why these types of guys were revered figures in the barrio. They were the real-deal bad guys who had done some really bad things. In our hood, as the rapper Ice Cube says, "...heroes don't fly through the sky of stars, they live behind bars."[1]

Without a doubt, growing up in this environment made me the cop I am. I grew up with direct insight into the criminal mindset, the family behind the criminal, the high-stakes games played, and how these gang members behaved and operated.

As a young kid, I saw firsthand the violence associated with bad guys, witnessing my first shooting at the ripe old age of about twelve. I say "witnessing," but it was more like "experiencing" because I had a front-row seat to a large fight that broke out at a family party, and guns were pulled. By the time I was fifteen, I had seen at least four shootings and had been shot at once. These events and happenings formed me as a person. I learned valuable lessons about situational awareness, planning and preparation, and reading people.

---

1. Ice Cube, "How to Survive in South Central," *Boyz N the Hood Soundtrack*, written by Ice Cube, Sir Jinx, Roger Troutman & Larry Troutman, released July 9, 1991, on Qwest Records & Warner Music Group, accessed June 20, 2022, https://genius.com/Ice-cube-how-to-survive-in-south-central-lyrics.

Looking back, I would say that reading people and situational awareness were probably the two key factors that made the biggest difference in making it out of this environment in relatively good shape. These two factors would also serve me well in my career as a cop because I still worked in the same environment, just from the other side.

I also attribute my ability to operate in chaotic and fast-moving environments to how and where I grew up. Having seen and been in the middle of at least a half-dozen highly-chaotic and life-or-death situations before even being old enough to have a driver's license no doubt helped hardwire my ability to do it as an adult.

Yet through all of that, I still saw the humanity in this environment because these were my people. These were the kids I grew up with and their families. So even though there was a lot of bad going on, I saw a different side to it. I think it still helps me to this day in how I view and treat even the worst of bad guys.

While I didn't really become involved in all of the neighborhood drama or politics at that age, I was exposed to it. Luckily, I had a very strong mother and extended family that kept me on the right track. My family balanced out the neighborhood and its poverty I was growing up in.

My mom and dad divorced when I was very young, and my mother was strong-willed and determined to make it on her own. This is why we were in government-subsidized housing in a low-income area. However, my family was middle class, and I spent a lot of time with my grandparents, who were small business owners and well off compared to my friends' families. So I had the luxury of experiencing and learning several demographics and classes of people through my formative years.

FARMING TOWN CULTURE SHOCK

Once I hit my high school years, we moved out of the inner city and into a small farming town on the far outskirts of the major metro area. This new environment was, without a doubt, a cultural shock for me.

The big-city problems were not there and neither was the big-city terrain I knew so well. Things were a lot slower, and there were no hard lines where I could or could not go based on the neighborhood. There was so much more integration already that it didn't have the importance it did in the city. I had to totally reconfigure my compass and "find my true north."

I mentioned before that in the city, you learn that who you grow up with or associate with might also determine who you could have friendships with outside your neighborhood. For instance, I played baseball on a Little League team, and several of my teammates were friends only when we played baseball. We didn't hang out much when we weren't playing baseball because our neighborhoods did not get along so well. For example, the players' big brothers might have been rivals, so the lines were drawn.

Now fast-forward to my new life in the small farm town. All of these boundaries disappeared. There were no boundary lines and no barrios per se. There were no real rivalries between any particular neighborhoods; hell, there weren't really even neighborhoods. It was such a small town that everybody just hung out with everybody else. The only separation was between the jocks (those who played sports), the cowboys, the stoners (smokers and drug users), and the nerds. Sometimes even these lines were all blurred.

One of the best things about my new environment was just focusing on everyday problems without the added stress of rival gangs and territories, which made life a little simpler. I left all of the inner-city problems behind and enjoyed just being a kid and having fun.

The second-best thing was that living in a small farming community meant that we could get summer jobs working on the local farms. The area was full of farmers, and potatoes and cotton were the two biggest commodities. So, when summer rolled around, most of us worked in the cotton fields picking weeds or in the potato fields on diggers and loaders.

The first summer I worked on a farm in my new hometown, I worked in the potato fields on a digger—a large rig pulled by a tractor that travels through a potato field and digs up the potatoes ready for harvest. The digger was a large, platform-type piece of machinery with an area where several of us would stand in front of a conveyor belt at about waist height. A scoop dug through the dirt under the potatoes, and then lifted the potatoes onto the conveyor belt.

The potatoes bounced along for approximately thirty feet on the conveyor belt. This bouncing action caused most of the dirt to fall through the conveyor belt, and just the large dirt clods and other big items remained with the potatoes. Those of us standing on the platform would have to take anything off that was not a potato.

At the other end of the digger, the conveyor belt

angled up at a 90-degree bend and eventually dumped into a truck traveling next to it. Once filled, these trucks returned to the potato shed, where the potatoes were sorted, washed, and loaded onto semi-trucks to travel to their destination. This was a continuous process all day and into the night.

We typically worked twelve- to sixteen-hour days on the digger. Usually, five of us manned the conveyor belt and ensured that only potatoes got past us. The job came with a few small hazards that I did not know about or understand at first—like occasional gophers, field mice, and the one I hated the most, the occasional snake coming across the conveyor belt.

At this farm, I mainly worked alongside migrant workers from Mexico. Working next to a person for many long and hard hours and having the common enemy of those damn trucks that came to get filled with potatoes exposed me to a unique perspective. Essentially, you are no longer white, Mexican, or other; you are just people doing a job and trying to make a living.

My girlfriend was Mexican, and her family lived and worked on the farm. So I primarily worked, hung out, and identified with Mexican people. I was once again fully immersed in Mexican culture. As a result, I was more fully exposed to the direct connections to the country of Mexico in our state.

Of course, this also led to a much deeper look into Mexican culture and a much better understanding of the hidden world of the narcos (the Mexican cartel drug runners). I worked and lived among a new group of people and was indoctrinated into a different part of Mexican culture.

My new friends and co-workers introduced me to famous Mexican singers, such as Vicente Fernandez and Ramon Ayala. I also heard my first corridos from the infamous Mexican group Los Tigres Del Norte. Corridos and "narcocorridos" are folk songs that tell stories of life for the Mexican people and the cartels' criminal activity. Many times certain cartel bosses or certain cartels are glorified within these songs (More about this is discussed in Chapter 4).

I gained an understanding that these were not just songs but actually stories told by people with direct knowledge of the cartel organizations. Stories that many of my co-workers could directly relate to.

These were stories about being of Mexican descent, traveling to a new country to make a better life, and often leaving family behind to do so. There were love stories,

stories of struggle, stories of betrayal, and stories of heroes.

At times, these songs had hidden messaging telling of the underworld of this life, the smuggling and the big bosses in Mexico who got a product—drugs or humans—into the United States. This is when I first learned that many people around me had family involved at all levels in the narco world of Mexico.

However, just like the gang members I grew up with, I knew these people as friends or associates. Even though they or their families may have been involved in the big drug world, I didn't necessarily see them as bad guys. I was living and working among them and saw them for who they were in that environment, not who they were in the cartel business. I had a unique perspective.

LAW ENFORCEMENT ASPIRATIONS

It turns out that my life from childhood through high school and into adulthood was, in fact, one big training ground for what I was destined to do. Without even realizing it, I was being trained on how to read people, treat people, and deal with people and their problems. How to read situations, detect danger, maneuver situations, and stay alive. I had no clue at the time what this would do for me later in life.

I did not know then that my life experiences would eventually provide me with a deep understanding of the very people I would later be fighting against for the sake of our county, our state, and even our nation.

As I finished high school and became a young adult, I felt it was time for me to choose what I wanted to be when I grew up. At the ripe old age of twenty, I applied to join the Sheriff's Office, and just before I turned twenty-one, I went to work in law enforcement. I knew in my heart that this was what I wanted to do for the rest of my life, and it was time to step into the arena.

I will take you through these journeys, this constant fight, and the real world hidden right in front of you. I hope you will walk away with a true understanding that this is a fight with real people and real struggles. This is a giant game of cat and mouse, but the stakes are much higher. In this game, lives are on the line. Everything we do and every move we make could be the difference between living or dying for those involved.

On the one hand, the issues are politicized and exploited by those on opposing sides. For those of us who work it and live it, however, we see the real people fighting this fight, real victims who are involved, and real bad guys with no conscience who are bringing the fight right to our doorstep—all in the name of money and power.

03.

LEARNING THE GAME

IT WAS THE SPRING OF 2000. The world was a different place, especially for cops and the military. The United States had not yet suffered the tragedy of September 11th, and as a young street cop, I was really enjoying myself and the job I was doing.

The 1990s and early 2000s were a great time to be a street cop. The world had not yet entered an age where we had instant access to cameras and computers in our hands. We also did not yet have the new phenomenon of Keyboard Warriors. People were still able to have face-to-face discussions and dialogue. Our society had not yet completely blurred the lines of good and evil.

I worked both in the jail and on patrol as a deputy before moving into my first assignment in what was referred to as a "specialty unit." A specialty unit is responsible for—and specializes in—a focused area of law enforcement. I was assigned to a unit that investigated traffic accidents, conducted drunk-driving investigations, investigated all fatal accidents in our county, and worked on drug interdictions on the roadways.

I had been in this particular unit for about three years, and while there were parts of this job I liked, there was some work I just did not care for. One of my least favorite duties was having to scoop up, bag, and process the broken and mangled bodies that went along with investigating fatal accidents.

There are things that you see and experience in these investigations that never leave your memory banks. Seeing compound fractures on a body where you wouldn't even think bones were present. Finding the teeth of a victim laying thirty feet from their body due to the violent nature of high-speed impacts. Looking at an entire human brain, perfectly dislodged and completely intact, as though it had been surgically removed after being forced from the skull by an impact.

There are also smells that never leave your memory. When you smell them again, they instantly take you back to the exact scene where you last encountered them. Unique smells, such as burning flesh, the iron smell of blood, the acid from broken batteries, and the weird and sweet smell of antifreeze.

Despite all of these negatives, I did enjoy other parts of the job, like the drug interdiction and the complexity involved with solving accident investigations. Some of these investigations included arresting and prosecuting criminals who drove under the influence of drugs or alcohol and killed someone in the accident.

While I was content with these assignments and was having fun doing it, I knew that I wanted to do other types of work in my field. With my background and experience, I was very much interested in working gangs and drugs. I felt that I had a distinct advantage in these areas with my early exposure to those things in my upbringing, and I felt that I could excel. So while I continued my work in the specialty unit, I knew where I wanted to head in my career.

During this time at our agency, the Narcotics Unit was run by a legendary sergeant, and his second-in-command was an equally legendary corporal. I had worked with the corporal before on our SWAT team, as he was an old-timer there as well. We had known each other and been on some operations together. Both of these guys were known for being no-nonsense cops and were well known throughout the cop world as being great narcotics cops.

The narcotics sergeant was allowed to handpick cops to work his squad based on who he thought would fit best. There was an understanding that not all people could work narcotics, so it was common practice to let the sergeant make his picks based on his knowledge and experience of the street cops. This latitude in selecting members to join the squad, combined with my working with the corporal in the SWAT realm, was about to open a whole new door for my career.

UNDERCOVER INVITE

It was an office day for me, and I was catching up on paperwork. In walked the narcotics sergeant and his corporal. The two of them said they wanted to talk with me.

The sergeant sat down and explained to me there were a couple of openings in the Narcotics Unit they needed to fill with some good cops. He wasted no time and jumped straight to business by asking me if I would be interested in joining them.

The question caught me off guard. As the question was posed, I thought they were talking about working in narcotics as a uniformed interdiction deputy. I thought I was a pretty squared-away, uniformed cop, and I wore a "high and tight" haircut straight out of the haircut scene from the movie *Full Metal Jacket*. I also prided myself on always having a crisp uniform and spit-shined boots. I looked every bit of a street cop. Hell, even if I were dressed in plain clothes, I did not think there would be any mistake in what I did for a living.

So, I asked the obvious question: Did they mean doing uniformed interdiction for the unit?

The sergeant quickly answered, "Negative," and said he wanted me to work undercover. Again, I was slightly confused because of my appearance as a uniformed cop. Based on my appearance, I would even get called "Robocop" by a few of the bad guys I usually dealt with. I brought all of this to the sergeant's attention, as I was genuinely baffled at how he expected me to do undercover work.

The corporal quickly jumped into the conversation. He leaned forward toward me, and in a low voice, he said, "Miklo, don't worry about that part."

The corporal had given me the nickname "Miklo," pronounced Mee-kloh, because of a movie called *Blood*

In Blood Out, in which a character named Miklo was a half-white guy growing up in a Mexican neighborhood. Because Miklo looked white, he was treated somewhat as an outsider. However, he grew up with all the guys from the neighborhood, so he was accepted into the Mexican culture and the neighborhood gang.

The corporal told me that I could be taught the undercover part. He explained to me that I had something that could not be taught: the background, upbringing, street smarts, and hustle to do the work.

He further explained that doing undercover work was more than just being a detective and doing the police work that goes along with it. He said, "Good undercover work requires a detective who understands the streets, understands the criminal mindset, knows how to navigate and deal with different people and cultures, and has the ability to stay calm and work through some tense situations."

With that, I said I was in and asked when I would start. Before long, I was a brand new undercover cop reporting for my first day of work in plain clothes. Looking back, this was the day I discovered a whole new world. I have to say, for me, one of the coolest parts of working undercover was the fact that I was expected to fit into the normal population. I got to wear regular clothes and drive a regular car, and I did not have to abide by the usual grooming standards.

Most uniformed cops often joke that when you go to narcotics (or "narcs," as we call it in our world), you have to grow a standard-issue goatee. This joke came from the stigma that male cops who went into narcs immediately grew facial hair, if for no other reason than that they could because of the relaxed grooming rules. So, I let my facial hair grow a little so as not to break tradition. Having pierced ears since I was about ten years old, I also put those bad boys in full-time. You know, to go all-in on the undercover role.

Driving a regular car as my work car was great. As a cop who was trained to observe, the ability to blend in among the normal population while working was eye-opening. It allowed me to watch how people behaved and see what went on with the criminal element when cops were not around. The ability to drive around without everyone knowing who you were wherever you went also made it nice to move around with ease.

PULLING BACK
THE CURTAIN

As I got trained up in the unit and started shadowing

some of the experienced narcs in the squad, my eyes were opened to a world I had been living in but was somewhat blind to.

I felt like Neo in *The Matrix* after he took the red pill and had his eyes opened to the real world. The surprising part was that I had seen some crazy shit as a cop, and I thought I was on my game in chasing and catching criminals. But it was not until I started working in the undercover world that I received true insight into the vast world operating behind the camouflage of everyday life. I started to see what a big world was behind the curtains and how the dope world connected to absolutely everything.

Of course, being in Arizona and bordering Mexico meant that anyone working in the counterdrug world had front row seats to the show (a.k.a. the fight against the Mexican cartels). Working undercover, I was not only watching the show, but my ass had a supporting-actor role in the middle of it.

In my work as an undercover, we did a lot of street-level work, which focused on quarter-bag dealers in neighborhoods. However, we also worked on the large-scale bad guys connected to the bosses down south in Mexico. The corner dealers were fun to work because, when you took them down, you felt a sense of accomplishment by having a positive effect on a neighborhood.

But working the cartels was a whole new level.

It is worth noting that, as local cops, we weren't even close to working these cartels like the federal alphabet soup of agencies. We dealt with the dudes who were at the lieutenant and captain level in the cartels, but the Feds were working the heads of these groups and the entire organization itself. Some of them even had their own corridos or tribute songs written about them.

These bad guys had complicated and intricate networks, and they were truly organized criminals in every sense. As such, we had to be squared away on our detective work. We had to be good at developing information and, more importantly, informants.

As I gained experience working in narcs, I got to do more and more. We were logging a bunch of surveillance time observing and reporting and only a small amount of time taking down bad guys. But it was this observing and reporting that made me better and better. The more time I spent watching bad guys operate, watching their habits, and learning their techniques and methods, the more I understood the game.

This is what it really boiled down to. We were playing one big-ass, cat-and-mouse game. But the odds were high in this game because the bad guys stood to lose a lot of money. And if they lost the bosses' money, somebody would pay for that. So, the game was very real for us all. We were playing for keeps, and our lives could be the price we paid. Something about your life being at risk—real, life-or-death risk—adds a whole new level to what you do and how you do it. The more I worked against the cartel crews, the more I understood their culture, beliefs, methodology, and how dangerous they were.

The exposure to the Mexican cartels taught me how interwoven they were with the Mexican culture. This was true on both sides of the international border, often called "The Line" or "La Frontera." La Frontera translates to "border," and The Line also refers to the actual international boundary between the two countries.

Most often in our area, we referred to the border between Mexico and the United States as The Line, and if you were in Mexico, you were on the "south side" of it. Many times, I asked informants about certain people we were investigating, and they would tell me that the person I was looking for was back on the south side. In simple terms, the person of interest was back in Mexico. Little nuances like this became important if you wanted to keep up in this game.

In this early era of my narc career, a certain stigma went along with the cartels. In Arizona, law enforcement dealt mainly with the Sinaloa Cartel, or CDS (Cártel de Sinaloa in Spanish). The CDS maintained a stronghold on our state and still does to this day. So on the south side, the areas containing the routes leading up to the Arizona border (also referred to as "plazas") were owned and operated almost exclusively by the Sinaloa Cartel.

Back then, the typical Sinaloa Cartel member was an old-school-Sinaloa-cowboy type. Cartel members would often dress in traditional Mexican cowboy gear, consisting of pointed toe cowboy boots, cowboy jeans, button-up shirts, and a Mexican cowboy hat, which had a very narrow and upward-bent brim.

You could get a sense of the status of a cartel member by their dress and how expensive their gear was. Those with higher status would have big, gold necklaces and medallions around their necks, gold rings on their fingers, and leather boots and belts made of ostrich and alligator. These guys looked like a cross between a Columbian drug lord and an old-western cowboy. No matter their look, one thing was for sure—they were running a big business, and they ruled with violence, fear, and intimidation.

One of the oddest things about the members of these

groups was that while they were violent and operated in a machismo fashion, they also stuck to specific rules and were very traditional in their beliefs and practices. Unlike the current cartel members, these old-school guys honored certain lines, such as leaving women and children out of their conflicts.

Of course, as the cartels progressed over time, this model changed as they became more overtly violent and crossed all previous boundaries. As they expanded to a worldwide operation, the cartel's exposure and work with legitimate terrorist organizations helped fuel many of their violent tactics. Tactics included skinning people alive, dismembering and beheading their enemies, and chopping off body parts after brutally raping and murdering women associated with, or connected to, their enemies.

04.

THE NARCO CULTURE

"TO ASSIST YOU ON our journey deep into the bowels of these criminal organizations, it is important that you know and understand the lifestyle. These organizations are so influential and prolific that they have created their own culture, commonly referred to as "narco culture."

We have to dive into the cartel belief systems, tools, and values. The goal is to provide insight into Mexican culture and discuss how the cartels have become a significant influence. You will learn how the Mexican cartels have hijacked the beautiful and proud Mexican culture and turned it into a violent and lawless subculture.

The cartels use their power and influence to break down and infiltrate every aspect of government and businesses within Mexico. I know that it is not a completely failed state, but I can tell you firsthand that the propaganda that the Mexican government has the problem under control is an illusion. The cartels have long-reaching arms and use bribery, blackmail, and violence to rule their world, and it works.

BELIEF SYSTEMS

I grew up Catholic and attended church with my mother and grandmother every Sunday, as did many of my Mexican friends. Catholicism is prevalent in Mexican culture, so it's no surprise that it also plays a dominant role in the cartel world.

The Catholic faith has many specific beliefs, saints, and customs. Many of these customs come into play with the Mexican cartels because, again, they have hijacked these practices for their purposes.

Take the use of candles for worship. There are candles with specific saints or prayers on them. We light them to worship or honor that saint and to request their intercession on our behalf. The saint can correlate to a specific area for these requests.

ST. JUDE

For instance, Saint Jude is considered to be the saint for lost causes. The St. Jude candle would be lit by a person desperate for help and include prayers asking the saint to intercede with God on their behalf. The cartels heavily prayed to St. Jude for this same purpose, but they would also ask him to protect them and help them get away with their criminal activities.

Often, we found St. Jude candles, statues, and shrines, and the cartel members had placed offerings to the saint. These icons would be high in the smuggling corridor mountains at the cartel scout hideouts. The offerings consisted of items like money, cigarettes, jewelry, alcohol, and drugs. Cartel members hoped that these offerings would please the saint, and the saint would intercede on their behalf.

Of course, the Catholic church neither practiced nor condoned this methodology. These criminals had implemented their own form of worship by using St. Jude to represent their causes.

This practice became so common that the true meaning of St. Jude often got lost. We talked to people who believed that St. Jude was, in fact, the saint who specifically helped the narcos by getting loads of drugs, money, or guns across the border into Mexico or just helping those involved in the drug game.

JESUS MALVERDE

Another example of the cartels mixing religion with their business was their creation of "narco saints," who are not actually saints.

The first and most prominent amongst the cartels—especially in our area—is Jesus Malverde. He was a pretty unassuming figure who looked like a young Chapo Guzman, the infamous leader of the Sinaloa drug cartel. He had dark hair and a strong, dark mustache, and he wore a white caballero-type shirt with black trim.

As the legend goes, Jesus Malverde was a Robin Hood figure when he was alive—a champion of the poor and oppressed. You see his image on shirts, hats, and jewelry. There are candles and statues of Jesus Malverde and some elaborate shrines honoring him as a narco saint.

Anyone can pray to Malverde, but the shrines are mainly used by those involved in the cartels. The belief is that Malverde will help protect the cartel members, their businesses, and their drug loads. The statues and shrines would have many of the same offerings I mentioned before, such as money, drugs, and alcohol.

SANTA MUERTE

Also very prevalent in this narco culture is the infamous Santa Muerte, who looks like a cross between the Virgin Mary and the Grim Reaper. This narco saint has a cult-like following and has satanic worship overtones mixed with Catholicism.

Santa Muerte is considered a female. People pray to her for protection from the police and revenge on enemies. She has become so popular in Mexican culture over the past decade that the Catholic Church officially came out with statements against worshiping her.

The worship of this narco saint has become prevalent in Mexican culture because of the cartels' influence. This popularity, in turn, has caused the younger generations to believe that she is an actual, legitimate saint. There are rituals and worship sessions to her that look like a cross between Catholicism and satanic worship. It seems both intriguing and scary at the same time.

POP CULTURE

Images and icons of Jesus Malverde and Santa Muerte were hands down the two most prevalent narco saints that we would find on cartel members. We would find them in the form of jewelry or prayer cards. Hell, we even ran into a few people who had tattoos of one or both. When you talked to these people and discussed Malverde or Santa Muerte, you could gain a sense of how they felt about them. They truly believed they were praying to a higher power for protection.

Believers in Malverde had more of a grounded view. They believed he was specifically looking over those who were less fortunate, those struggling to make it, and those who had to turn to crime to make a living. They believed that Malverde would protect them if they worshiped and gave offerings in his name because he understood their struggles.

But Santa Muerte had a range of believers. Some believed she simply watched over those same types of people believed to be protected by Malverde, but others worshiped in more of a satanic cult that performed blood rituals and pure evil in their worship.

Either way, if we came across people who had anything bearing the pictures of the two, we immediately knew where they stood and what side they were on.

The only problem was that these two "saints" also became almost pop-culture images in Mexican culture due to the cartels' influence. So we would find people—specifically those in the younger generations—who idolized the cartels and sported these images because it made them seem cool.

TECHNOLOGY AND PROPAGANDA

Another significant cultural influence was the rise of technology and social media, which helped spread cartel propaganda worldwide very quickly.

Using the internet became vital for the cartels to conduct an all-out war. They used platforms such as YouTube, Facebook, and Instagram to flaunt their status, riches, drugs, weapons, beautiful women, and exotic animals. They also documented their world travels, their nonstop flow of spending cash, their large, Hollywood-type parties, and what seemed to be their luxurious lifestyle.

All of this, of course, immediately attracted the younger Mexican generations. It had a Kardashian Effect in tricking these youngsters into thinking that these drug lords were living such great lives.

The cartels used these platforms for psychological warfare and propaganda as well. They issued challenges to rival cartel members, made videos mocking their enemies, and documented their violence toward rivals with videos of interrogations and executions.

They used their money and power to gain a technological advantage by either hiring or extorting experts in the field. They used this same technology and the ever-increasing use of cell phones to track their enemy's movements. Social media platforms and cell phone usage allowed them to track one another and conduct kidnappings and murders.

Tracking became so prevalent that the cartels increased their online security at lightspeed. They also completely changed their standard operating procedures concerning their personal security and typical online activity. The revised procedures helped protect them from each other, but it also made it harder and harder for us in law enforcement to keep up.

NARCOCORRIDOS

The cartels further bolstered their social media presence by using the ever-popular "narcocorridos." These folk songs tell stories of infamous cartel members and glorify the cartel life. They would be played by the cartel members and those who look up to them.

Corridos have been around forever, but the narcocorridos of today are much different.

The older style of corridos were tales of hard times, personal struggles, and lost love. They contained only somewhat hidden messages about the cartels, which were not yet even referred to as cartels. I would listen to these old ballads myself while growing up. You had to decipher the hidden messages to understand the stories being told about the narcos.

The narcocorridos of today, however, are much more sinister and violent. They contain blatant challenges to rival groups and descriptions of how they will kill and mutilate one another, or they graphically detail past battles and assassinations. These songs are much more like the gangster rap world, where playing and listening to these songs can incite violence.

The cartels take this propaganda created through music, video, and social media very seriously. In fact, there has been a new phenomenon in which the person or band singing the narcocorrido is held responsible for songs they sing in favor of a particular cartel or cartel boss. So, if someone sings a narcocorrido favoring one specific cartel, the rival cartel may threaten or even kill him.

INFILTRATING THE MEXICAN CULTURE

As you look at all of the puzzle pieces to this complex narco culture, you can see how the cartels have created a subculture within Mexican culture. Mexico could be considered a failed state or on the verge of being a failed state. This situation directly results from the Mexican cartels' extreme violence and ability to corrupt their government leaders completely.

As a powerful machine controlling both the government and the people of Mexico through violence, they also influence with propaganda and bribery. This heavy influence has solidified the cartels' power and position.

All in all, the cartels are powerful and dangerous organizations that have corrupted the entire country of Mexico and parts of the United States as well. The fight against them is real, dangerous, and constantly evolving.

Many of the operations I will talk about are from several years back, and the cartels have since changed tactics and techniques. They conduct their business, get disrupted or intercepted by law enforcement, learn from this, change their methods, and continue forward. Change is constant because they are driven by money, greed, and power, so this is not a problem that will diminish anytime soon.

The stories in this book demonstrate what the fight looks like from my perspective as a cop on the street. But as you go through each chapter and each operation, keep in mind that this is not normal. It's not normal for a county agency like mine to have to adjust to military-type maneuvers and operations to counter an organized group of criminals on this scale.

Organizations like cartels are usually investigated solely by the larger federal organizations, like the Drug Enforcement Agency (DEA) or the Federal Bureau of Investigations (FBI). Our county and our agency were in a unique position in that way. We worked against these criminals directly and even had some of the cartel members living in our county. This is one of the main reasons that these experiences are so unique.

Left: A Santa Muerte candle and Santa Muerte cloth pendants.

Right: A Jesus Malverde hat from a load vehicle.

A cartel shrine located at a stash house in Pinal County.
The shrine has a combination of legitimate and narco saints.

A Santa Muerte statue and a Santa Muerte picture located at a cartel stash house.

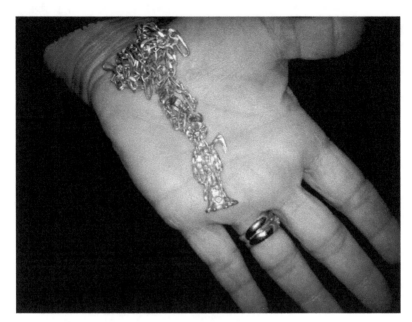

A Santa Muerte pendant from a cartel scout.

A shrine at a smuggler's house with St. Jude, Virgin Mary, and Santa Muerte statues, and sage.

05.

THE F'ING NEW GUY (FNG)

IN MY NEW ASSIGNMENT as a narcotics detective, I gained more experience, was involved in more operations, and started to understand my role better. Like in any new job, I had to assimilate into my new tribe of co-workers, earn their trust and respect, and prove that I had what it took to do the job. Anyone working in the narcotics world has learned what I was learning and has been there themselves.

I quickly discovered this dope game had some long and strange hours, and there was no real sense of proper business etiquette for drug dealers or smugglers. This was especially true when it came to keeping appointment times or even having appointments during regular hours. There is something called "doper time," which is the most random and abstract form of time on earth. Doper time means there are no set times or rules for meetings, deals, phone calls, or text messages.

What doper time boiled down to was this: shit would happen when it happened. So, I could set up a deal to meet with an informant or a dealer at, let's say, four o'clock in the afternoon. With doper time being the rule, the meeting may not happen until five or five-thirty. Hell, sometimes it wouldn't happen until whenever they decided to show up, which could be hours later. This took a little getting used to, coming from a paramilitary structure in the cop world.

Who am I kidding? This shit drove me nuts. At first, I would constantly check my watch and ask the rhetorical question, "Where the hell is this guy/girl?" I had to get real comfortable with learning how to just chill and hang out for a while until my contact showed up.

Doper time was just one of many little things I had to learn to deal with as a new narcotics detective. How well I adjusted and how well I did all the other aspects of the job determined how little or much work I did as a detective.

As I advanced in my narcotics career, I continued to

learn, and learn, and learn some more. I felt like I was progressing fairly well, starting to get my feet on the ground and my "sea legs," as they say. Honestly, I would say I was probably even a little cocky at this point.

I had done a few street-level deals that went okay, I had put together some cases on bigger targets, and I had been on a few good cases. I enjoyed the work, and with the amount of learning I was doing, this was by far the best assignment I had ever had.

I had even gotten somewhat used to the phone calls when the boss said, "Cowboy up, puto," which sounded crude at first, but I later realized he didn't mean for it to be offensive. His translation was, "Pluck up your courage, Matt. We've got work to do."

The hard part about this assignment was just the long and random hours. I was married with a kid, and I was living two lives. I would go in for a regular shift and work ten hours or so, then get home to eat some dinner and hang out with the family. Inevitably the phone call would come, and I would have to get back to work.

That is the other part about this work—it doesn't stop. There are no business hours or days. It just happens when it happens. So when an informant calls and says, "Hey, a shipment is coming through," you have to scramble and get resources together to try to intercept it or land it at a location, or whatever the plan is for that particular crew and their dope.

My family often made much more of a sacrifice for this job than I did. I was doing the easy part. I would just answer the call, get my gear, and go to work. My wife was left running the household, taking care of the kid, and wondering if and when I would make it back home.

We don't talk about this part of our job too much because it sucks. We try to justify the fact that we are up and out because we are fighting evil and bad guys, but it really does take a special person to be the spouse of an undercover. There are late-night phone calls and text messages. At times, you get up in the middle of the night, get dressed, and take off, not wanting to wake everyone up. So you slip out like a kid running away from home.

But all of these things add up. Everyone doing the work makes the same decisions and sacrifices and under-stands exactly what it takes to succeed. This is where you "earn your stripes", as they say. This is where you prove what kind of narcotics detective you are and prove your worth to the team. I did all of these things, allowing me to move forward and get better at being a narc.

I knew that I had finally been accepted into the fold

when I got included in some bigger cases. All of those late-night phone calls to come back to work were starting to pay dividends. The time you put in essentially becomes a vetting process to prove your abilities, dedication, and will to do this work.

This vetting process moves you forward, and you earn more and more of the types of cases and work you want. Well, I should say that *some* want; like in any other job, certain people thought they were built for it but were not. So I was continuously working a case, proving to the bosses that I could handle it, and then moving up in responsibility and case complexity. As I continued that process, I fell deeper in love with this kind of work.

Then one day, my corporal called us all in to brief us on a case we were working. As with every other case brief, he told us who our targets were, their background, and what type of operation it would be. For this operation, we played the role of a marijuana supplier with Mexico connections.

We would be the organization making the delivery of the marijuana to the distribution point. In this particular case, we were pretending to be an organization from the southern part of the state, and we would be delivering the drugs to the Phoenix area.

Here in Arizona, the two big distribution points are Tucson and Phoenix, and typically speaking, the farther the drugs are from the border, the more they are worth. You see, the danger to dope smugglers transporting drugs is that they can be intercepted along the way, either by cops or by "rip crews," which are essentially robbery crews who focus solely on stealing drugs along transport routes. (I'll talk more about rip crews in Chapters 7 and 13.)

The corporal gave us our assignments, and I learned that my role would be that of a transport driver. This was a big deal for me because it meant that my bosses trusted me to handle a role like this. I had to be on my game because the transport driver played a somewhat important role. I had to pay attention to what I was doing and not allow myself to get robbed along the route. I also had to ensure that I didn't get stopped by the uniformed police.

I would essentially be running a clandestine, or covert, operation with an assumed name and no police identification or anything like it. As a transporter, I would also have to pay attention to the people I was dealing with to ensure that I was not driving into a trap of any kind. Sprinkle in just a little more pressure of being an undercover cop, and I was basically playing the acting part of my life to ensure that those I was dealing with were comfortable that I was not a cop. So, again, to me, this was a big deal.

While we were briefing, I got my marching orders and all of the available intelligence at the time. I also learned my role—who I was to the bad guys (or who they thought I was). I found out my fake background and then went through a series of questions and answers to ensure that I had replies to possible questions the bad guys could ask me. Last, I found out the other team members' assignments, instructions, and security protocols I had to stick to on my route.

The plan wasn't too complicated. I was a solo driver of an SUV loaded with "fresh packs." These were the backpacks of marijuana transported on foot by "packers," which was short for backpackers. These backpacks typically had anywhere from two to four bundles of marijuana. (I'll cover the packers' role in more detail in Chapter 7).

Each of these bundles averaged around twenty pounds, with some a little heavier and some lighter. The packs I would be transporting weighed right at about fifty pounds each, and I would be transporting six of them for a total of about three hundred pounds of fresh Mexican marijuana. It was a huge load, and it held a street value of approximately $150,000.

As the main undercover detective responsible for

setting up the deal finalized the last-minute details with the buyer, we ran through equipment checks. We also ran through some possible scenarios with each other just to ensure we were on the same page. Then it was time to "cowboy up," as they say.

This operation would be pretty simple as far as these deals go. I would drive the dope to a specific location, wait for my cue, and then deliver it to the buyer at the location specified by my undercover. My undercover was a Mexican detective playing the role of a connected-cartel guy who was selling his product to the Phoenix market.

For the sake of business, we ran the most risk transporting the drugs to Phoenix from Tucson. As such, we were able to set a good price with minimal negotiations on the buyer's part. After all, the Phoenix market price was always pretty set, so there wasn't much back-and-forth negotiating, and the only time you got better pricing was when you moved more weight.

It wasn't long before the undercover said we were good to go, and we started our operation. I had my gun, a push-to-talk phone, and three hundred pounds of marijuana in the SUV I was driving. I got on the interstate at a location between Tucson and Phoenix and began my trip to the meeting spot in Phoenix.

I had a chase vehicle following me in case I encountered any problems along the way, and I planned to both give and receive updates along the way. As I entered the main area of Phoenix, I would be given instructions on where to exit and where to park and wait.

Everything was going smoothly for the first part of the trip. I was getting updates and check-ins from both my chase vehicle and the undercover.

But about 10 miles outside of the southern part of Phoenix on the interstate, I noticed that I had not seen or heard from my chase vehicle. As a matter of fact, I had not had any communication from any of my team in what seemed like an eternity. So, I jumped on my push-to-talk and tried to raise my chase vehicle. Nothing. Then I tried raising any other members on the push-to-talk network. Nothing again.

I passed a Highway Patrol sitting in the median, and he looked like he was doing drug interdiction work. It was then that I became really nervous and thought to myself, *Shit, if he pulls out and comes after me, I am going to jail.* My thoughts were racing, my heart was pumping, and I was frantically trying to raise one of my team members on the radio.

You know how you slowly top out on a hill while you

are on a roller coaster, and then right as you start the downhill side, your stomach drops, and your adrenaline dumps? That is exactly where I was at this point. All I could think was that I was going to get pulled over by a uniformed cop, and I had nothing on me but a gun, a phone, and 300 pounds of the Sinaloan's finest marijuana in the back of the SUV.

This radio silence went on for about ten very long minutes that seemed more like two hours. Then, suddenly out of nowhere, a voice yells out on my push-to-talk, "Miklo, Miklo, you got a good copy, Miklo." I was never so relieved to hear my corporal's voice. My corporal was also in the chase vehicle, so I knew they were somewhere close by.

Needless to say, I was a little stressed at the current situation, so I yelled into the phone, "Where the fuck are you guys?"

My corporal came back with a little giggle in his voice and said: "Settle down, Miklo, we've been with you the whole time. We just lost you for a minute."

He then instructed me to take the next exit and then get back on the interstate in the opposite direction. I followed my instructions, but quite honestly, I didn't know why the hell I was turning around. As I got back onto the interstate, my corporal told me that I needed to return to base. The deal was off for now. While I did not understand what was going on, I knew that this was not the time to ask a bunch of questions, so I drove the load back to our starting point.

When I pulled into the office, a whole crew of detectives was standing around outside and talking. As I parked and got out of the SUV, the laughter and the jokes started. My corporal asked through his laughter if I was alright. I said I was, and I began to feel like this may have been a setup just to see how I would perform.

As I walked closer, the laughter settled into a few small chuckles, and the corporal told me that I did fine. They assured me that this had been a real deal. The buyer had found another source just before we got to Phoenix and had called it off.

Now, while I know that this happens, I still cannot help but think that this was all a test. But if it was indeed a test, I had not failed. While I did get a little amped up, I stayed on course. I had the added luxury of some extreme stress for a few minutes, but I didn't allow it to take me off of my mission.

I will never truly know if what happened was actual or if it was a test. Nonetheless, I made it through. Moments

like this operation enhanced my experience and my confidence that I had chosen the correct career path.

These moments were the real-life pop quizzes that we
got in this job, where no amount of preparation could give
us every tool we needed to get through it. Sometimes we
just had to do what we thought was right. Hell, sometimes
we had to make this shit up as we went.

06.

GETTING STRIPES

IT WAS EARLY 2001, and I was still loving my job as an undercover. I picked up an announcement that indicated that our agency would be testing for the position of Sergeant. I talked to my wife a little about it and thought it would be good for me to go ahead and take the test. It would give me some experience for when I was actually ready to promote.

The thing is, you never really think you are ready to be promoted, so you test "for the experience" as a way to work past the doubts. I was having way too much fun to leave narcotics, but I knew that I would be ready to leave at some point. And I knew that I only wanted to do that by promoting out.

I always made sure that I looked at the long game, and for me, the long game was to be promoted to sergeant one day and then work my way back as the sergeant over narcotics. I wasn't arrogant enough to think that I was ready, but I knew that I would have several years working as a sergeant to prepare for it. So, I bit the bullet and took the test.

Whenever I tested for a position, I went all-in on it. I never did anything half-assed, and if I went after something, I went after it one hundred percent. I was still pretty young in tenure. I had been with the agency for almost eight years. At that time in the agency, most of the people promoted to sergeant were on the job for ten years or longer.

When I looked around, though, I knew that I did not want to work for certain people, so part of me wanted to make sure that I held the same or higher rank to avoid that. And another part of me knew that the only way I could affect more change was to promote up. So, I went into the test with the attitude that I was the best one testing and did not have anything to lose, even though I knew that I did not want to leave narcotics yet.

Much to my surprise and dismay, I came out at the top of the list. I was surprised because I had had some solid competitors in the testing process, and I was dismayed because I was not ready to leave my current gig.

Not long after I had gotten the results, I got a call from the sheriff congratulating me on my test scores and letting me know that I was up for promotion. The choice was mine to accept or decline, and the sheriff gave me a few days to think about it.

This same sheriff had worked undercover himself. He had also been promoted up the ranks, so he knew what an internal struggle this was for me. His only advice was to do what was right for my family and me. He was always a great leader, and he continues to be my friend to this day.

Once I had this phone call, it was time for me to set up a meeting with my narcotics sergeant and let him know what the deal was. I started by telling him that I was thinking of turning it down because I really enjoyed the work I was doing, I enjoyed working for him, and I didn't want to leave the unit.

My sergeant told me to sit down. He proceeded to give me some of the best advice I have had to date for my career path.

He told me that he would not allow me to turn it

down and that I had a bright future. He talked about missed opportunities and how second chances for those rarely come along again. Then he left me with the fact that I could always come back to narcotics, but it could be as the sergeant.

In this meeting, my long-game vision kicked me in the head, and I knew what I had to do. I took the promotion and spent the next few weeks winding down in narcotics, turning over my case files, contacts, and informants. Once I had successfully handed off all of my workload and cases, I left the unit and moved back into uniform and into being a shiny new sergeant in Patrol.

I immediately recognized that I was a much more savvy patrol guy after just the brief exposure I had to the undercover world. The things I was exposed to and experienced in my short stint in narcotics had given me a whole different perspective and view. I had a much deeper understanding of the world's undercurrent—the behind-the-curtains view—and it made me a better cop and a mentor for the younger members of my squad.

Another good thing that went along with this promotion was that I maintained my position on the SWAT team, so I still got to fight the cartels from time to time in a way that I loved.

As a uniformed sergeant, I continued to learn and grow not only in leadership but in my knowledge of the cartels, the culture of the cartels, and everything they are connected to. I sent myself to as many classes as I could on Mexican cartels, the drug game, and gangs to study my opponents and learn as much as possible.

I also maintained contact with my narcotics corporal, and he schooled me on the cartels that operated in our area. He told me about operations he was involved in. I am pretty sure some of them were not sanctioned by our agency and didn't take place in the United States, from what I could tell. But that is all a story for another time.

All of this helped me in my everyday duties of being a street cop, but it was also helping my long game. As I knew it would happen eventually, the Narcotics Sergeant job became available in 2007, and this was my shot. The current narcotics sergeant was moving to another role, and I was now positioned to take his place.

When this job comes open, it is filled much like the narcotics detective positions—there is no announcement, no testing process, and it really comes down to your experience and name. By your name, what I mean is your reputation. Your reputation as being knowledgeable, confident, calm under pressure, and a leader are just some of the traits that can get you a shot at this spot.

The sheriff generally selected the candidate who would fill this position (with input from some of his command staff under him). This was the case for me, as I got the phone call to meet with the sheriff to discuss the Narcotics Sergeant position.

When I met with the sheriff, he explained the importance of the position to the agency. Further, he explained the reasoning behind the very exclusive selection process. He also explained the importance of the job to the county, the state, and the country. The sheriff acknowledged that our county was integral in the larger fight against drugs.

You see, people often think that local cops only focus on local problems like the corner dope dealer. While our Narcotics Unit did investigate these cases, we were also unique because we had key Mexican cartel members living and operating out of our county. And as I mentioned earlier, our county was significant terrain for these same cartels in their billion-dollar business. So holding the position of sergeant on this squad was an important role.

The sheriff then dove into the uniqueness of the budget and administrative portion of the job. The administrative duties were critical to the continued success of our Narcotics Task Force, as it was a federally-funded and also multi-jurisdictional task force. He explained that the responsibilities I would assume would be unlike any other sergeant in the agency because of this. The fact that I would oversee a large budget, interact with command-level staff from across the state, work closely with the federal agencies, and manage staff from several different agencies assigned to the task force made this position unique.

After the sheriff had laid out his expectations, he asked if I was ready to take the job. My answer was absolutely yes, and I had been preparing myself for this exact moment. I excitedly accepted the position and thanked the sheriff for his confidence in me to do it.

My new position started an all-out transformation that I did not expect. I did not fully understand the level of the fight happening against drugs and the Mexican cartels that push them. I knew what the job entailed, but I had no idea of the battle I was about to jump into or the long hours and days ahead of me.

I would be moving into what had become a full-on war against the Mexican cartels. While I had kept myself educated on the cartels and the drug game, this would be a complete look behind the curtain, and I would learn more than I think I ever cared to know about these ruthless criminal organizations.

07.

CLOAKED IN CAMOUFLAGE

I **WANT TO HELP YOU UNDERSTAND** how the cartels are structured. The easiest way to give you the layout of these organizations and how they operate is to describe everything we have to deal with in fighting these groups, breaking down all of the different cells and how they operate. To do this, I will work backward, starting from the ground-level members and working up, so you can understand and envision how the cartels are structured and how each group works in the grand scheme of the organization.

As you have seen in previous chapters, the operations

themselves look very much like a combination of military maneuvers and law enforcement tactics and techniques. This shocks many people. Law enforcement in the United States does not usually deal with issues such as these—especially using the tactics we used to combat this problem.

The shock factor comes from discovering that these operations occur right here on American soil. And, they often extend well into the interior of our country, not just along the border itself. As I said before, the world is cloaked in camouflage, and most people do not know, do not understand, or do not care about what is actually going on all around them.

THE COMMAND STRUCTURE

To understand the battleground, you have to realize that the Mexican cartels have a very elaborate structure and a command and control system in place. At times it can be very rudimentary but still very effective.

Their command structure is similar to a paramilitary system, with bosses in Mexico at the top who have complete control of the organization. Below these cartel bosses are what would translate to captains and lieutenants in charge of specific branches of that cartel, and there are cells within each branch.

Each cell has its own function but sometimes functions in more than one area. A cell could be responsible for logistics, enforcement, security, transportation, distribution, manufacturing, and many other aspects of operating a multimillion-dollar criminal organization.

As you work your way down the organization's structure, you find that there is always a good level of control by the top bosses as to what each subordinate group is involved in and how they operate.

Like any business or organization, you will also find that as the individuals or small teams become specialized and efficient with their assigned duties, the job assignment will be unique to them. That small group may be the only ones performing that work within the organization because they are good at what they do.

However, unlike typical businesses, these organizations are involved in illegal activity. Members of this organization who are not good at their jobs or make mistakes can be disciplined—and even lose their lives.

THE PLAYERS

I will cover most of the groups we deal with in our fight, but please understand that this will not cover every piece of these vast organizations and their web of activities.

I will talk mainly about human and drug smuggling and some of the organization's money laundering and firearms smuggling activities. But, the cartels are involved in much more than just these crimes.

They are known as Transnational Criminal Organizations, which means that their criminal tentacles reach worldwide, engaged in everything from counterfeiting to kidnapping to oil theft.

THE TRANSPORTERS

The first group we will discuss is the transporters, consisting of pilots, backpackers, and vehicle or ATV drivers. They either fly, backpack, or drive drugs from the U.S.-Mexico international border north into the United States.

"Flying" refers to people who fly ultra-light aircraft specially crafted and rigged to hold several hundred pounds of drugs. "Backpacking" refers to humans carrying loads of drugs on their backs for the five to six days it takes to travel on foot from the U.S.-Mexico border into our county.

When we refer to the "driver" transporters, this is just what it sounds like—people driving vehicles. Let's look at the drivers a little more closely.

DRIVERS

Drivers fall into three distinct groups for our purposes. Some try to drive vehicles with hidden compartments across the official border checkpoints. Others drive trucks that have been stripped down and loaded with drugs to try to sneak them across the border. The third group carries loads of drugs through the rough desert terrain on ATVs.

HIDDEN-COMPARTMENT TRUCKS

Some cartel drivers simply drive vehicles with very sophisticated hidden compartments through the official points of entry.

These compartments are generally structural changes to the vehicle to create a void. They can fill these chambers with drugs headed northbound and weapons, money, or ammo headed southbound. The compartments can be welded-shut voids or can have hydraulic mechanisms that open up to reveal the hidden space.

The drivers running the hidden-compartment loads through the entry points were a lot different from the other two types of drivers, and typically, their driving skills were not their most important skill. Their biggest strengths were remaining calm and blending in like chameleons to avoid detection.

We worked some of these drivers on our interstates, but generally only as part of very large cases. Our guys and gals who usually worked them are called "interdiction officers." These officers were trained to recognize and apprehend these drivers.

DESERT LOADERS

The second type of drivers are the people who drive vehicles, usually stolen and fully loaded with drugs, across the border and north into the U.S., avoiding the official points of entry. They also make return trips to Mexico—sometimes loaded with guns, ammo, or money, and sometimes empty—to be quickly reloaded with drugs for another northbound trip.

They cross into southern Arizona through border areas with no barrier fence, or they do what we call "ramping" over the areas with vehicle barriers. The barriers are small posts like those you see in parking lots, and they typically stand about four to six feet high. They prevent vehicles from simply driving across the border, but there is always a way to defeat anything if you have the time and money.

The cartels have specially-developed ramps placed on each side of the barriers, creating a makeshift bridge over the top of the obstacles. Vehicles can then drive from the

Mexico side, ramp over the barriers, and continue right into the U.S. side with ease.

Most drivers we dealt with and chased were these ramping drivers, driving what we call "desert loaders," which are stolen or cartel-owned vehicles loaded with drugs and driven from Mexico into our county.

I have to tell you that I was often quite impressed with the driving skills of some of these guys, and I feel that they could have easily been top-notch Baja race drivers had they chosen that profession. I have been in some open-desert car chases with these guys that were reminiscent of the old moonshine car chases during prohibition days. I have witnessed firsthand some of these drivers, driving in complete darkness with no lights through the middle of the desert, be able to outrun or outmaneuver us in a chase.

The desert drivers also had some clout or street cred, as it applied to their position in the organization. Often, they would be mentioned by name or nickname in the narcocorridos, which is a big deal because it proved they had standing and respect for their work in the organization.

One additional note on these drivers, and sometimes their one or two passengers, is that they had some serious flat-tire-repair skills. We have watched these guys get a massive tire leak, stop, repair, and get rolling in less than three minutes. It was like watching a NASCAR pit crew. We often joked that if these guys just put their skills to use for good rather than crime, they could do great things.

As we worked operations to interdict these drivers, they learned from their mistakes. When we tracked them by their tire tracks and intercepted a drug load, they learned to use carpet covers on their tires to cover their tracks.

They also visited the local tire shops where Border Patrol had their vehicles serviced to see what types of tires the Border Patrol used. They then used the same tires for their smuggler trucks. This would make anyone tracking the tire tracks believe that they belonged to Border Patrol rather than the smuggler vehicles.

ATV

The third group of drivers worth mentioning drives all-terrain vehicles (ATVs).

The cartels recognized that the ATVs were a middle ground between backpack crews and full vehicle loads. We had become very efficient and effective at intercepting the full-size desert loaders. As we honed our skills at setting up, chasing, and intercepting vehicle loads, the cartels began to shift their tactics. They knew that backpacking the drugs on foot took longer, and the loads were significantly smaller. So the ATV drivers came to be. While a vehicle load would run anywhere from 1,500 to 2,000 pounds of tightly-packed marijuana, an ATV load would typically run from 200 to 400 pounds.

These loads were a little tougher to interdict because the ATV's dexterity and ability to travel over rough terrain made it difficult to chase them unless we were also on ATVs. An advantage for the packer crews was that they could hide and wait—or hide and avoid—law enforcement if they encountered them along their journey to their final destination. When a full-sized vehicle load encountered law enforcement, it was easier to run as their loads were small, but the cartels knew that they would lose the entire load of drugs when they got caught. The drivers would usually get away, but the cartel did not care about their drivers; they cared about their commodity.

The ATVs gave the cartels the ability to move these smaller loads quickly and efficiently. It took more of them to get the same amount of drugs that full vehicle loads could deliver. But using an ATV made it easier to hide the drugs and run, leaving the drugs in an area under the watchful eye of a scout while the packers acted as decoys to draw us away from the drugs.

You already know and understand the terrain we are talking about here. This is the remote Arizona desert with a spider web of mesquite- and palo verde-lined washes and culverts that run north to south.

When we have our summer monsoon rains in the Arizona desert, we can get several inches of rain within just a couple of hours. With the hard and dry desert floors, this rain barely soaks into the ground. Instead, it collects in and travels quickly down every crevice in the desert floor. As the water begins to puddle and make its way south, these small crevices become tributaries that feed the larger culverts and washes.

The fallen rain then becomes full-on raging, muddy streams of water that will fill a twenty-foot-wide creek bed bank-to-bank and several feet deep. This turns into the local flash-flood phenomenon, where a creek bed that is dry for 98 percent of its existence becomes a raging river that knocks down thirty-foot trees, rolls two-ton boulders down the river, and will quickly lift and take away a full-size truck at lightning speed.

But 98 percent of the time, these washes are dry, and they provide a dirt- and sand-filled path with a canopy cover of thick mesquite and palo verde trees along the banks. Many times, if you are walking through or standing in these washes, you can see only pieces of the sky as you look up through the branches and leaves of these trees. You can look ahead and behind, and it gives the appearance that you are inside a tree-lined tunnel, with plenty of spots along the way where the water has eroded the bank, providing small caves that act as sanctuaries.

All of this makes these washes ideal for traveling undetected. A dry wash provides cover from aircraft and drones overhead and from people sitting on hills close by who may be watching the area.

Being the ever-changing entrepreneurs of illegal activity, the cartels started to exploit this situation. They would pack 300 to 500 pounds of drugs on the front and back cargo racks of the ATVs (which most of us know as "quads"). Then the driver would transport these drugs on the ATV through the open desert using the same smuggling corridors and the over-watch provided by their scouts.

As they pushed north into our county, they would travel on both the open, four-wheel-drive roads and trails that the full-size trucks used in these washes. If they were traveling in the open and the scouts notified them on their smuggler radios that law enforcement was in the area, they would quickly drive into the closest wash and either hide and wait or continue to travel under cover of the trees blanketing the wash.

If we located them and attempted to take them into custody, they would flee on these ATVs and use the terrain to their advantage. The ATVs could use routes that our vehicles could not. Or they would simply go off-road and take the smaller and more agile ATVs into rough areas where we could not follow.

Then, as they reached our county, they would most often pop out from the open desert into local farm or horse-property neighborhoods, where an ATV really didn't look too out of place. Of course, these ATVs were loaded with large bales of drugs and generally had a driver decked out in camouflage. Nonetheless, the sound and sight of an ATV going by did not arouse much suspicion.

Cartel members would drive these loads right into a local stash house, unload the drugs from the ATV, provide the driver with a bag or two of supplies, and send him back south through the same routes. The driver would make supply drops for the scouts as he traveled back to the international border to collect his next load of drugs. Then, he'd do it all over again.

This method of transport became one of the more difficult ones for us to interdict because of the agility and speed of the ATVs and their ability to travel into rougher terrain if we chased them. In addition to this, they would use countermeasures to help them cover the routes they were using.

As you can imagine, if they were using one particular route with these ATVs, the tracks left behind were very distinct and easy to track. To counter this, the ATVs would drag a large piece of weighted-down carpet behind them. This technique would erase all signs of foot or tire tracks and make it very difficult to track anything.

As effective as they were using the ATVs, we eventually figured out ways to disrupt and interdict them. Fortunately, when we intercepted a quad load, we usually got both the driver and the vehicle with the drugs on it. The ATVs also became a great way to identify stash houses by watching this activity in the local neighborhoods, which was an unintended benefit for us.

SCOUTS

As I've briefly mentioned, the cartels also have "scouts." The scouts are guys who are in place at key locations from Mexico all the way up to our county. They are basically lookouts who work on the mountaintops, the open terrain, on local farms, and sometimes are even mobile in vehicles.

The scouts utilize communication systems that can be as simple as mobile phones and as complex as professional-grade VHF radios, complete with rolling encryption and signal towers located throughout the terrain. This provides the lookout network with real-time communication with each other, the transporters, and the bosses running the show. It is an efficient way to observe and control the terrain they use as their smuggling routes.

MOUNTAIN TOPS AND VALLEY FLOORS

Most of the scouts we dealt with were either on mountaintops or in the open desert areas. At the high point of smuggling activities in our county, we believed that there were upwards of 100 scouts lined throughout the mountains and open terrain, from Mexico and through the seventy miles north into our county.

These scouts would be in place—essentially camping out—for weeks and sometimes even months on end, depending on how much activity there was by the cartels. Their camps would be very close to their actual work location (wherever they would have the best vantage point to view the areas they were responsible for watching over).

In military terms, a mountaintop location is called a "listening post/observation post," or LP/OP. A cartel LP/OP would be where the scout or scouts would sit, watch, and report on their areas of responsibility.

If you have ever been to the mountain ranges in southern Arizona, you will understand how much of a vantage point these LP/OPs provide. We have large and steep mountain ranges that shoot up from flat desert valley floors. These LP/OPs would typically be on high peaks or peaks that gave the best views. You could literally see hundreds of square miles of open desert valleys below you and to the next mountain ranges.

Of course, each strategic mountain range would have scout coverage or presence, so scouts could see each other's LP/OP positions and maintain overlapping fields of view. This overlap allowed the scouts to have excellent control over the area, and they could observe and report any activity.

The communication systems they maintained also meant that they did not have to be on watch constantly. When there was cartel activity, the bosses would notify everyone to get into place and be ready. The broadcasted announcement was an indication that there was planned activity by the cartel, and the scouts needed to start paying closer attention.

It's important to understand that the scouts were held responsible for the product in their area. If a scout on a hill had a load of drugs coming through his area, he had to pay close attention and provide information to the transporters and bosses. If the scout missed something for some reason and a load of drugs or other contraband was intercepted, the scout was responsible for that failure and the loss.

The punishment could be as simple as withheld wages until the loss was covered or as complex as being sent to Mexico to explain the failure. The latter usually meant that this particular scout was never returning from Mexico. Being called back south by the bosses usually signified that he would not live much longer.

At night, the scouts would sometimes shoot military-style flares into the air that slowly floated back to the ground. The flares not only sent a signal but also lit up quite a large area of the terrain. In this way, scouts could signal other scouts, drivers, or packers without using their radios to indicate something was going on in their sector. They also got a good look at the desert terrain to try to spot any law enforcement, unauthorized people, or vehicles in their area of responsibility.

It was a little annoying to spend time and energy

sneaking into an area, only to have a scout pop a flare and either give our position away or cause everything to lock down. Sometimes we would use this tactic against them. We would pop our own flares to make everything shut down and force all of the scouts in the area to focus on one specific spot. Then we would use this distraction and sneak into other locations. Sometimes we would use this tactic just to confuse the hell out of them and disrupt their activity for the night.

CAMPSITES AND EQUIPMENT

The scouts' campsites and equipment are worth covering to help you understand how rudimentary yet sophisticated these cartels were.

The cartels understood that law enforcement utilized air assets (usually helicopters) to search for and counter them. So the scouts used or built small cave-like structures on the mountaintops. They would take a small void in an area of boulders, heavy brush, or trees. They would build around it using rocks and brush to form a nice makeshift structure that blended in well and was often very hard to detect.

These structures became the scouts' living quarters. The scouts spent their downtime in the living quarters, using them to sleep, cook, and hide if air assets or law enforcement were in the area.

Scouts had sleeping bags, food, water, extra batteries, clothes, weapons, ammo, and other supplies to maintain life and carry out their duties in their camps. We would find high-quality binoculars, camouflage clothing, ammunition in heat-sealed plastic bags, weapons, cell phones, professional-grade radios, car batteries, solar panels, canned foods, camping stoves, dry foods, alcohol, cigarettes, and religious candles.

Some of these items make sense given what the scouts were doing, but others needed a little further explanation.

WEAPONS AND AMMO

First, we will touch on the weapons and ammunition. To properly understand why the scouts were armed since they were essentially hidden and just observing and reporting, you must understand another critical piece of this smuggling game.

Robbery is a phenomenon in these open-desert areas in our county. There are groups of people referred to as "rip crews," short for rip-off crew or robbery crew. They understand that a load of drugs is most vulnerable to being intercepted during transport. (This is also why the drugs gain value the further north into America they go. For instance, a pound of drugs at the U.S.-Mexico border can gain up to a 150 percent price increase in Phoenix.)

These rip crews would sneak into the smuggling routes and hijack the transport load of drugs. They would then make the short trip from our county into the Phoenix Metro area with the drugs, where they would repackage and sell them at a premium price.

A rip of one backpacker crew of marijuana could yield the rip crew anywhere from 200 to 500 pounds, which equated to approximately $100,000 to $250,000 of profit for minimal work and literally no investment. The scouts carried weapons and ammunition specifically to address these rip crews. The scouts were expected to spot and counter anyone they suspected of robbing the drug loads.

The scouts also understood that having weapons in their possession would equal longer jail time if law enforcement caught them. So, to have firearms and ammunition available but hidden, they would seal the ammo, and sometimes the weapons, in plastic bags and bury both in or near their campsites or scout nests.

CAR BATTERIES AND SOLAR PANELS

Now, about the car batteries and solar panels. The

scouts' professional-grade radios, much like our police radios, operated off of rechargeable batteries specific to these radios. In addition, the scouts had regular GPS-type radios that hunters or hikers commonly used. And there were cellular phones on some of these mountaintops.

Of course, there was no electricity on mountaintops or in the open desert to charge or recharge any batteries needed for these devices. So, to overcome this problem, the scouts hauled car batteries and solar panels up to their LP/OPs.

These solar panels and batteries provided a constant trickle charge to the car batteries. The scouts would then hook up the radio and phone chargers to the car battery bank, which was anywhere from two to six car batteries linked together as one large energy source. They would use this bank of car batteries to keep multiple phones and radio batteries charged and ready to go, ensuring that the scouts maintained the ability to constantly communicate as needed and providing them with a constant mountain-top supply of electricity.

The first time I found car batteries sitting at a scout camp high up in the remote hills of the Arizona desert, I thought that those scouts must have lost their minds on drugs. Who in the hell would tote those things up these hellacious hills, and why? Once I figured out what they were doing with them, I realized just how ingenious these guys could be.

RADIOS

The cartels' radio system was sophisticated. In the mid-to-late 90s, the radios used were basically the same as ours, but with older technology. So they were using the same type of radios, but they would use unsecured VHF frequencies that we could pick up using normal scanners. The cartels and scouts would openly communicate their radio traffic over these radios, and we would be able to intercept the transmissions with our scanners.

The problem was that they would use their own code system as well. Rather than talking just plain language, the cartels would mix it with codes they had created. These codes were known only to them, so we would have to filter through radio transmissions and piece together the information to determine the conversation contents and context.

We often found that their codes were created using nicknames of landmarks, people, or places. For instance, they might refer to the "window" when talking on the radio but would be referring to a hilltop that had a natural rock formation with a hole in it. Obviously, the term "window" would be very difficult to figure out without context.

As time went on, the radio technology got better. When the cartel discovered that we were listening in on their radio conversations, they were able to upgrade better and more secure systems. How they found out that we were listening in could be a chapter of its own, but let's just say that even in U.S. law enforcement, sometimes we had operational security problems.

As we moved into the early 2000s, the cartel radio systems started using simple encryption, but they would not use it full time. So, sometimes the transmissions were unencrypted and were what we called "in the clear," and we would still be able to pick them up on scanners. When the cartels used encryption, it made listening to radio conversations a little more challenging, but we still managed to find ways to intercept them during our operations.

Fast-forward a few years, and the radio systems moved from VHF to digital, which effectively wiped out the ability to use a high percentage of typical scanners. This digital switch again raised the difficulty level of listening to their transmissions, and we had to work with radio techs on our side to figure out workarounds.

As we continued forward into the 2010s era, the radio

technology continued to advance, and the cartels began to use professional-grade radios that were both digital and had rolling encryption. We were essentially unable to intercept transmissions using traditional means, and the only way to hear them would be to have one of those radios.

The problem with getting a cartel radio was that they used passcodes to unlock them. They also maintained a pretty good accounting of these radios. The passcode protection meant that even if we could get our hands on a cartel radio, it would lock once it was turned off. When we turned the radio back on, it would require a code to be entered on the keypad to unlock it.

Let's just say that cartel members were not the most cooperative when you asked them for things like a radio passcode. So we could no longer count on radio interception as a viable method to interdict the shipments or catch these bad guys. We did figure out a few ways to get it done here and there, but it was becoming rarer.

If you understand these professional-grade radio systems, you also know that there must be a repeater system or radio towers for the system to be effective for the distance covered by the cartels. They did, in fact, erect and maintain their own radio towers on U.S. soil, from

Mexico up to the outskirts of Phoenix.

These were not the traditional 300-foot-high towers with the mandatory red lighting to warn planes of their presence. These were rudimentary and small radio towers erected just high enough to not stick out like a sore thumb while providing the much-needed radio signal transmission.

There weren't many of these, but they were out there, and they reminded me of just how sophisticated and organized these cartels were. I mean, really, a radio system with repeaters lined the desert from Mexico to Phoenix. It pissed me off when their radios worked in places that mine did not, but that is a whole different story.

LOGISTICAL SUPPORT GROUPS

Besides the scouts, there were the logistical support groups. We can break these groups into radio tech support, vehicle supply, drug load pick-ups, and scout supply.

These logistical support groups became a battle in their own right as we tried to disrupt their ability to operate and communicate effectively. We could have easily overlooked these groups if we were not paying attention. They often looked very ordinary and blended in with typical, everyday activities going on in the world. We had to pay attention to their movements and patterns to figure out exactly what they were up to.

RADIO TECH

The first of the logistical support groups, the radio techs, is a pretty cut-and-dry group. The cartels had these radio techs on payroll, and they were responsible for maintaining the cartel radio systems and radio towers. They would program the systems, keep inventory, and maintain the overall radio network and system.

The technology was just as advanced as our police radio technology. The radio techs for the cartel were masters at keeping their system running, keeping the inventory up to date, and maintaining both the radios and the system itself. Having technicians to maintain and run these different types of radios and radio systems was a key to their continued success.

VEHICLE SUPPLY

The vehicle supply group was responsible for stealing vehicles in the U.S., which, for us, meant mainly from the Phoenix Metro area. They would then take these stolen vehicles directly south through our county, primarily utilizing the smuggling routes, and cross them into Mexico for use as transport vehicles.

During the high point of this activity, they liked to steal and use full-size, four-door trucks and full-size SUVs. They were very efficient at stealing these vehicles. We would often be chasing a stolen truck in our county before the owner even realized their vehicle had been stolen.

DRUG PICK-UP

The drug pick-up crews consisted of people hired to go to a location to pick up drugs, people, or both, and transport them to a stash house. Where they went after the pick-up would depend on who their direct boss was and what they were transporting. Generally speaking, they picked up the drug backpacks or bundles from the crews that had walked the drugs up to our county from Mexico.

The people doing these pick-ups would sometimes be locals in our area or from the Phoenix Metro area. Sometimes they were people involved in the drug game as regulars, and sometimes they were people who had never done this type of stuff. The cartels had recruited them with the promise of making easy money for simply driving the load from our county to Phoenix.

These pick-up crews had to be careful, though, because

they too were subject to the rip crews that would hijack drug loads. The rip crews would outfit their vehicles with red and blue lights and pose as law enforcement, making traffic stops on these transport vehicles. Of course, they would then simply hijack the drugs or even the whole vehicle.

SCOUT SUPPLY

The last logistical group is the scout supply group. These people bought, transported, and delivered supplies to the scouts in the desert and on the mountaintops.

They would go to local stores and purchase canned foods, tortillas, cheese, lunch meat, chips, water, alcohol, batteries, cigarettes, cell phones, small propane tanks, and any other supplies that the scouts might need or request. They would put the items in large, heavy-duty trash bags and then transport them through the smuggling routes.

A member in supply would drop off the goods at predetermined locations and signal the scouts, who would then walk or hike to the drop location to get their supplies and take them back to their LP/OP and camp locations.

The scout supply crews would make these same runs week after week to ensure that the network of scouts had what they needed to survive in their assigned locations.

Some scouts made out better than others—we sometimes would intercept not only alcohol and cigarettes but also prostitutes who were hired to take care of the scouts' carnal desires.

EATING AN ELEPHANT ONE BITE AT A TIME

You should now have a decent insight into the ground-level groups of the cartels that we dealt with and battled against. As you can imagine, the ground-level fight had many different facets.

At times we would have to focus specifically on one particular group to have a positive effect, rather than focusing on the whole organization. Actually, this was probably true most of the time. We would focus on one particular aspect, like going after backpackers, interrupting scout supplies, or chasing down stolen vehicles. It was easiest to attack it this way because to attack the organization as a whole would have taken many more resources than we had as local law enforcement.

We did work with federal agencies from time to time on very large-scale cases, where we would work the organization as a whole. But these tended to be cases that got drawn out over months and even years. As the local law enforcement agency, our goal was to eradicate these bastards from our county and push them out. So we focused on the smash-and-grab type operations—we worked whatever angle we could to capture them and their drugs and put them behind bars.

Most of the time, we were operating on dual planes. We had detectives involved in the large-scale and lengthy investigations that focused on the organization as a whole. At the same time, we had ground-pounders who worked interdiction details, chasing the loads, the scouts, and the resupplies.

We all worked hand-in-hand. The interdiction teams provided all of the intelligence gleaned from our operations to the detectives to add to their investigations. When the detectives got actionable intelligence, they, in turn, gave it to us to go out and smash bad guys.

A cartel scout carrying a handheld radio, wearing all camouflage clothing and carpet shoe covers.

A fully loaded SUV containing multiple bundles of marijuana.

Backpackers carrying a backpack load of marijuana.

Smugglers on an ATV loaded with re-supply items for scouts.

Weapon, ammunition, and radios at a cartel scout camp.

A scout cave with the entrance covered with rocks and sticks to hide the location.

Marijuana bundles discovered hidden in the brush on one of the smuggling routes.

A cache of scout radios used by the cartel scouts.

Trash located at a scout cave, evidence of the scouts living in this location for extended periods of time.

08.

KITTING UP

IT WAS THE FALL OF 2007. The heat had finally broken for our brutal Arizona summer, and the nights were finally cooling down to the low 70s. I was going through an equipment check at home, which generally included prepping food and water for the night and getting all the necessary gear together.

Weapons checks were first and foremost. I ensured everything was operational on my issued Glock pistol and Colt M4 Commando. The rifle was my primary weapon for these operations.

In 2007, many companies made rifles on the AR-15 style platform, but our agency and team liked and ran the Colt rifles. Our team still had some "old-timers" who preferred the Colt platform because that was what they were used to. These guys were comfortable with the Colt short barrel .223 M4, so we remained loyal to it.

Next, I looked at the gear necessary for the upcoming night's work. I checked the function and battery level on my PVS 14 "NODs," or night observation devices. These NODS had two eyepieces that fit right up against my face. Both of these fed into one tube facing away from me and converted the images so I could see in darkness.

My NODs were mounted on my "skull crusher," a device that fitted onto my head like a cap. It allowed me to wear the NODs and use them hands-free. The only downfall to this skull crusher was exactly what the name implies: It put a lot of pressure on my head to hold up the weight of the NODs, and it gave me a headache within five minutes of wearing it every single time.

We wore the skull crusher with NODs attached when we drove into our assigned areas of operation and when we were on foot, moving or watching an area. Some guys had started using bump helmets, which were basically tactical bike helmets that were much more comfortable to wear, and we could attach our NODs to them instead of using the skull crusher. These were much nicer to use but did not offer any ballistic protection. They only protected us from bumps and bruises on our heads.

The military was always ahead of law enforcement in this type of gear because soldiers fighting wars overseas were using their equipment at a whole different level of bad-guy chasing. But people did not understand that we in law enforcement were doing many of the same things our soldiers were doing overseas. We just did it much less efficiently and with equipment that was a generation or two behind our military technology.

So, we slowly caught up in technology, and through a program in which law enforcement was allowed to get used military equipment, we got better and better gear.

Last on the equipment checklist was my plate carrier and all the gear carried on it. The plate carrier is essential-ly an over-the-clothing vest with molle loops that allow you to mount different pouches and accessories all over it. Inside the plate carrier are rifle-rated ballistic protection plates. The plates could take hits from a rifle round and were bullet-resistant to these rounds.

On my plate carrier, I had a bunch of accessories mounted, including my extra pistol magazines, extra rifle magazines, IFAK (Individual First Aid Kit), "soft" (or disposable) handcuffs, a flashlight, a navigation light, and my issued portable radio.

In addition to all my gear, I always made sure I had my "go bag" ready. The go bag was a basic 5.11 tactical backpack filled with protein bars, water, an extra IFAK, mosquito repellent, binoculars, extra batteries, basic over-the-counter meds, and a GPS/radio combo.

I learned to carry all this stuff based on my needs during past operations. For instance, I quickly discovered that mosquito repellent was an absolute must due to the amount of aggressive and hard-biting mosquitoes that came after me in the rugged Arizona desert.

Once I had completed my full gear check and had everything ready, I loaded it in my specially designed four-wheel-drive Tahoe. This was not your typical cop SUV. Chasing these particular bad guys resulted in many extras being added to our vehicles to ensure we had the capabilities we needed for our mission. Many of these extras are still used today, so I won't get specific. But let's just say it was a sneaky ride.

Next, I did a quick run-through on my vehicle and the vehicle-mounted equipment. This check always included a roll of black electrical tape. Operating in complete darkness was another fact of life in this game, and you would not believe how many little lights there are in a vehicle. The tape was the best way to completely cover any interior lights I did not need or want visible for the operation at hand.

About two hours before dark, my family was preparing to sit down for an earlier-than-normal dinner. Making adjustments for me to work abnormal shifts and schedules allowed us all to eat together and have some sense of a normal life.

Earlier, I mentioned "doper time." When you fight against drugs and those pushing them, you work on their hours and their terms, which were random at best and had no rhyme or reason. Anyone who works in the fight against drugs knows that deals and operations often happen in the most inopportune times.

You could have just finished a twelve-hour day, gotten home, and peeled off all of your gear when you get the call that it is time to "mount up" and get back out there for something that has come up. That "something" could be an informant tip that a load of drugs was moving, a street cop that made a traffic stop on a car that had a load of drugs, or a person who got arrested for something and wanted to give up information in exchange for their temporary freedom.

As we finished our dinner and caught up on family business, my mind started to wander to the night ahead. I began running the latest intelligence briefings through my mind, combining these with debriefs of bad guys and the information they had given. I played the chess match in my mind to decide what the next move would entail and the ripple effect it may have.

It was usually during this time when my mind shifted that my wife would tell me that I "changed." She said it was almost like I would become another person, getting very quiet and disengaged. I didn't even realize when I was doing it, but she was right.

To start getting ready for work and mentally prepare for the night ahead, I would "put on my game face." This game was real, and if you were the loser, you or others could be hurt or killed. That's why I had a laser focus on the job I had to do and why I went through a mental checklist while I showered and put on the day's uniform. I knew that once I walked out of the door of my house, it was game-on. And from that moment forward, the game was life or death.

Once dressed and geared up, I made a few final checks, spent some last minutes with the family, and headed out the door. Typically, I had at least a 45-minute drive to the spot where we would all rally up to brief for our nightly operation. I used this time to run scenarios through my head. I also took the time to process our plans, assess team member assignments for the night, and ensure we had all of our spots covered.

I got updated intelligence briefs and talked to the senior sergeant to discuss our plan. I was the newly-assigned sergeant over this squad, and I was shadowing the sergeant who was leaving the team.

He was old school and, in fact, was the same guy who introduced me to the narco game back in 2000 when I had first been recruited to work undercover. I had some big shoes to fill, and I had a lot of learning to do. I was confident I could do it, but I also wanted to learn as much as possible from my predecessor on running this squad and running these operations.

It wasn't long before I arrived at our predetermined location for a briefing. We discussed assignments and got to work. Little did I know what this night would bring and how much being prepared would count.

09.

THE FIRST RODEO

AS THE EVENING APPROACHED, I pulled into the briefing location to meet with the current unit sergeant. He was training me to take over the unit as the supervisor. I jumped out of my truck and gave the sergeant the customary handshake and quick hug. He gave me his usual greeting, "Qué onda, Miklo?" ("What's up, Miklo?")

We were the first ones there by design. We needed to discuss the operation without interruption so he could lay out his plans and assignments for the night.

These operations were more complex than they appeared, with many moving parts and angles that had to be covered. Usually, the planning would occur after phone conversations or with quick, in-person briefs to decide how to move forward. That decision was almost always based on intelligence gathering, information from confidential informants, increased activity levels observed in the smuggling corridors, or a combination of all of these.

The cartels don't take days off, so there was always something going on. However, we had to get the best bang for our buck. Having limited resources and manpower, we couldn't just go out blindly all the time and hope for the best. The sheer vastness of the smuggling corridors made it like looking for a needle in a haystack. Add in the fact that there were scouts for the cartel scattered from our county down to Mexico. It made enforcement action tough without intelligence and information on cartel movement to work from.

As we discussed the plans for the night, the sergeant asked me if I would prefer to shadow him to see how he supervised the operation or if I wanted to take a worker position within it. To understand the reasoning behind this question, you must understand the culture of a squad or unit such as this.

These specialty units are always a little more tightly knit than your average detective or patrol squad. Don't get me wrong—any team that works together regularly has a bond and good camaraderie. But units like narcs work under more extreme circumstances. This, in turn, creates a group of people who must have a high level of trust in one another. Part of creating this trust is getting to know one another, working operations together, proving your work ethic and abilities, and working well under pressure.

As the new supervisor, my answer to what assignment I wanted was easy for me. I would take an operational assignment as a worker rather than shadowing a supervisor. It was vital for me to understand each of these roles if I was going to put people into these positions and supervise them. And it was important for my team to be confident that I knew what I was doing and that I could and would be willing to do anything that I would ask them to do.

I also didn't want to disrespect the team's loyalty and dedication to the outgoing sergeant by trying to insert myself as their new supervisor. Minimizing my ego and taking a secondary role as the outgoing supervisor finished his time with the unit was much more well-received than acting like a bull in a china shop to establish myself as the new leader.

In these operations, there were several types of assignments. We had ground assignments where you were on foot. There were also vehicle assignments, within which there could be several different roles. Each role was important to the overall safety and success of the operation and was integral to interdicting the bad guys.

The ground assignment where you were on foot was considered by many to be more difficult. It was hot during the summer and cold during the winter. You were out in the elements and exposed to bugs, insects, snakes, and any other animal or nuisance out there.

Generally, you would ride in a vehicle to a drop point where you would be dropped off with your gear. These drop-offs would happen covertly so scouts in the area wouldn't be alerted that someone was there and watching. Once at the drop point, you would make your way to your assigned location on foot.

Typically, the assignment would be at or near the smuggling trail or roadway the smugglers were using. Depending on whether we were after backpackers or vehicles, your job could vary from observing and reporting, to deploying tire deflation devices (spikes), to being on a takedown and arrest team. You could also be designated as a listening post/observation post (or LP/OP), which usually meant that you would have to do a little hiking to get to higher ground to be in an overwatch position.

For a ground assignment, you would load your gear into a vehicle, usually driven by one of the team members assigned as a vehicle unit. Your equipment would usually consist of the usual stuff, like your primary handgun, rifle, and ballistic outer carrier vest with all the necessary attachments like extra magazines, med kit, radio, and handcuffs.

You would also have your bump helmet or ballistic helmet (skull crusher), night-vision goggles, and tire-deflation devices (if needed). You also had a backpack filled with water, food, extra med supplies, a global positioning system (GPS), a small camp stove to make instant coffee, bug spray, and a military poncho liner to use as a cover or as a pad to sit on.

Sometimes you would have some extra gear with you, like different technologies used to detect and locate smugglers. But I won't get into those specifics because some of this technology is still used in the fight against cartels today.

After getting dropped off at your pre-designated drop point, you would hold your position to acclimate to the area and ensure that there were no bad guys in the vicinity. After a bit, you would communicate your position and status and proceed to your assigned location.

Once there, you would report to the supervisor and acclimate yourself to this new position before setting up your gear. After you're situated and fully operational, you would give a final check-in via your radio to let your supervisor and the rest of the team know you are ready.

Then it would be time to sit and observe. You would maintain your position, report any activity you noticed, and allow the supervisor to determine how the team would act on any information or observations you gave.

Some of us would have surveillance assignments, which were essentially the same as the ground assignments, except you would be in a vehicle. While you didn't get exposed to some of the elements and critters, it was also a little more challenging to hide a truck, so you had to be crafty and creative to outmaneuver and outwit the scouts and load drivers.

The surveillance vehicles would also often be designated as rescue vehicles for the ground team members. So, if the ground team member encountered any trouble in or at their position, the rescue vehicle would roll in to help. The other assignment for vehicles was the takedown or chase vehicle. They would pursue the bad guys. Generally speaking, this was a coveted assignment. It meant you would be in a vehicle, protected from the elements and critters. And when the smugglers showed up with their load, your sole function in life would be to take them down and arrest them. Of course, the bad guys would flee on many occasions, so you would also be the team chasing the smugglers as they attempted to get away.

READY FOR THE HUNT

For our operation on this night, I chose the ground assignment. To me, this was just like hunting. I would have to sneak into the areas where my prey lived and operated. Then I would have to locate and observe my target and determine the best course of action to ensure that I could get close to or intersect with it. Lastly, I would make my move to take down my prey.

To me, there was no better hunting than to capture these bad guys, but my prey was often armed. To paraphrase Ernest Hemingway, there is no hunting like the hunting of armed men. Knowing that this would be my assignment, I prepped my gear as we awaited the arrival of the rest of the team.

As the team arrived, we greeted each other, and as was the custom, we cracked jokes and even did a little smacktalking to one another. We were showing our fellowship with and endearment to one another. I know that sounds counterintuitive, but when you do this type of work, you understand that humor masks some apprehension about the ever-present dangers and the possibility of death that is always lingering close by.

When the greetings and smack-talking were out of the way, we got down to business. The sergeant called everyone's attention. He briefed us on the latest intelligence and what the operation entailed that night. He then called out assignments and reviewed who would need what equipment based on their role. We learned who we would pair up with and who would ride together to the assignment location.

Once this was complete, we went through a brief-back, where we each repeated back to the sergeant what our assignments were. This time was also our opportunity to ask any clarifying questions or make any adjustments. Then we got our departure time and broke to prepare and load up our equipment.

Typically, we would be given a specific time that we were expected to be at our final assignment area. Since the unit had done these operations previously, we knew the travel times for both the vehicle and on foot. This allowed us proper travel time from the briefing area to the final location, with a small window of time built in to stop and get gas, drinks, or any other last-minute items.

It was still a little warm on this particular night, even though the summer heat had started to break and the nights were cooling down. The temperatures were in the 80s and 90s (rather than 105 degrees at midnight). Storms had also rolled through a day or two prior, which helped keep the dust and crap in the air down to a minimum.

However, this also meant higher humidity for us. When you live in the Arizona desert, the dry heat is a real thing. We typically have very low humidity, and when storms come through, they raise the humidity to a level we are not used to. Now, what we consider humid is laughed at by those who live in regions with high humidity, but it still affects us because we are so used to the dry heat.

The other phenomenon related to the rain and humidity is that these conditions seem to be a super-attractant for mosquitoes. I'm not talking about normal mosquitoes either. These are legit, Arizona-desert mosquitoes that seem to run in packs of one million. We are used to operating in an environment where everything bites, stings, or sticks you, but these things only come out for a short period during the summer, and I think they try to make up for lost time by draining you of as much blood as possible.

Because of all these factors, good bug spray is an absolute must. So, as part of my preparation for that night, and knowing that I would be on the ground in an area thick with these pests, I made sure to lay on the repellent pretty thick before gearing up. I also ensured that I had my head net to keep those little bastards out of my face and ears. Anyone who has ever been exposed to mosquitoes knows exactly what I'm talking about. They seem to have a particular love for your ears, nose, and mouth for some reason.

I then loaded up with my partner and ride for the night, who was a good friend and fellow SWAT team member before being assigned to narcs. I threw my gear in his small truck, and we headed to a local gas station to gas up and grab a couple of cold drinks.

We headed out to our assigned location, about twenty minutes away. As we drove, we caught up on family stuff and reviewed the night's plan. We specifically discussed our exfiltration plan and medical evacuation procedures in case something went wrong and I got shot or injured while on the ground assignment. These conversations may not seem normal to those outside of this job, but they were a reality for us and completely necessary to increase the odds in my favor should something go wrong.

It wasn't long before we got close to our final assignment location, where it was time for us to disappear. We were entering an area where the cartel scouts were present and watching, so we needed to look like regular civilian traffic going into that area. We would also use the terrain, horse properties, or random structures to "black out." We would be driving with no lights from that point forward.

As we prepared to go dark, we donned our skull crushers with our NODs (night vision) attached and then began to sneak into the heart of the smuggling corridor. We often had enough information to counter the scouts and either avoid them or travel through without getting their attention. But they were damn good, and it was no easy task to sneak through this area. A cartel scout works for some pretty bad guys, and if a scout screws up at his job, he won't get a write-up or a bad review—he'll get a beating. Or worse. So, they were pretty motivated to do a good job and watch their areas closely.

After sneaking in for several miles, we reached my drop-off point. We slowly came to a stop. I jumped out and grabbed my gear, including my rifle, backpack, and spikes. I turned on my radio and conducted a quick radio check to ensure it was working correctly.

I then gave my partner a quick hand-slap and knuckle-bump and began moving on foot to my final location for the night. During daylight hours, the area was on a fairly well-traveled road. However, later into the night, local traffic on this road became almost non-existent. Then the cartels could come out of the desert-smuggling routes and make their runs on this route to get to the local stash houses.

This is why my ground assignment was both necessary and vital. I would be the first one to see a load vehicle coming through, verify that it was, in fact, a load vehicle, and then relay information to the rest of the team to prepare for and conduct an interdiction.

That was the only part of the assignment that really sucked. Once I relayed that information and the team prepared to intercept the load vehicle, I had to stay exactly where I was and listen to the team chase and apprehend the bad guys, all while I sat in the desert and just listened to it happen. I didn't get to be involved with the takedown.

As I mentioned earlier, at this time in the smuggling game, the cartels preferred to run their drugs in full-size quad-cab trucks or full-size SUVs, mostly stolen out of the Phoenix area. These vehicles would be stolen from hotels, businesses, and residences in the Phoenix Metro area and driven south into Mexico to be fully loaded with drugs. They would remove damn near everything except the driver seat and pack it full of drugs.

The cash crop was marijuana for the Sinaloa cartel, so this is what they packed. The dope was typically compacted into twenty- to thirty-pound bricks that were about three feet wide by eighteen inches high by two feet deep.

The compact marijuana would usually be wrapped in a heavy foil and then covered with several layers of brown packing tape. Sometimes there would be additional layers added in that would contain everything from transmission fluid to coffee grounds to try to cover the odor of the marijuana inside. The outside of the packages would always have markings that signified which cartel they belonged to or where the drugs came from.

As I walked toward my assigned location, I adjusted to walking with night vision on. This may sound like a somewhat easy task, but I guarantee that walking with night-vision goggles on is much harder than it sounds. My particular night vision was a PVS 14 model, which started with two tubes and two eyecups that sat against my eyes. The two tubes filtered into one tube at the front, so it looked like a small pair of binoculars at one end that turned into a monocular on the other end.

A few things happen when you wear night vision

that makes it a little more challenging to function while wearing them.

First off, you have a narrow focus and lose any possibility of peripheral vision. Just imagine looking through binoculars as you try to walk and function, and you will know what I'm talking about. Now, add darkness to that.

Also, the only night vision we had available displayed a darker green picture, so when you looked through these devices, everything appeared as shades of green. Darker objects and shadows appeared as a darker green, while lights and lighter objects would appear as a light green. You had to translate the darker and lighter colors to hills or rises and depressions or dips on the ground in front of you.

The amount of ambient light played a role in night vision. If it was a nice moonlit night, it made operating under night-vision goggles much easier than if there were no moon or ambient light.

So, I carefully walked through the wide-open desert toward my final destination. Growing up in the Arizona desert, I always appreciated being out in the middle of the night when it was the calmest and quietest. There is something cathartic about walking in silence while the sounds of packs of coyotes howling echo in the distance and the many other sounds of the desert surround you.

The air was starting to cool. From the recent moisture, I noticed the ever-present smell of the greasewood bushes. But there is another distinct sound in the Arizona desert this time of year that you hope you never hear up close: the rattle of the many different species of rattlesnake that inhabit this area. It was always in the back of my mind.

While I was trying to move covertly, I was also trying to create enough vibration from my footsteps to act as an early warning system to any rattlers in the area. I hoped they would return the favor by firing off their rattlers as a warning that they were close.

Luckily, with my night vision tech, a rattlesnake's eyes look like two little, shiny emeralds glowing in the dark of the night. They were very subtle in their appearance, but once you had seen them and understood what they were, you always knew exactly what you were looking at when you saw them again.

Fortunately, I did not encounter any of our scaly friends on this trek. As I arrived at my spot, I quickly set my gear down and scanned the area to ensure that I was not sharing any close-proximity space with bad guys or unwanted critters like skunks, snakes, or scorpions. The area looked clear, and I only shared my space with the regular clusters of greasewood bushes, small palo verde trees, and a few saguaro cactuses.

I arranged my gear in a cluster of small bushes and trees to properly conceal myself from any passing vehicles or the rare person on foot. I then quickly prepped the spikes for deployment, and I staged them in place to be able to launch them rapidly on a vehicle when the time came.

These tire deflation devices were made to deflate both regular tires and heavy-duty, four-wheel-drive tires. This was important because most of these stolen vehicles ran on heavy-duty, four-wheel-drive tires.

Remember, the cartels would purchase bulk amounts of a specific four-wheel-drive tire that just so happened to be the same tire our brothers at the United States Border Patrol used on their Border Patrol vehicles. So, as the stolen vehicles made it south into Mexico, they would put on the new tires. The cartel would use the same tires as the Border Patrol to throw them off. They would try to make it look like it was the track of another Border Patrol vehicle, hoping that the agent would discount it as another good guy.

They did this because they understood that the men and women of the U.S. Border Patrol were some of the best ground trackers in the world. The Border Patrol tracked so often and in such volume in our area that they could look at a tire track, identify the tire's brand, sometimes the tire's size, and the direction of travel.

Once my spikes were in place, I got on my radio to advise the sergeant that I was ready. Other team members did the same until we all confirmed we were in place and ready. We were now operational and ready to intercept the bad guys.

Meanwhile, the sergeant gathered the latest intelligence, checked in with some informants, and got any information he could to ensure we were in the right area to intercept the bad guys. The sergeant notified us that our route was on the agenda tonight for the bad guys, but there was no specific time frame. Now it was a hurry-up-and-wait situation.

As I settled into my position, I once again swept the area for any invading critters. Seeing none, I made a nice spot against a small tree to lean my backpack on, and I sat down and leaned back against it to watch the road.

The road ran south onto an Indian reservation and continued south, connecting to other roads that eventually led all the way down to the U.S. and Mexico border. There were also several off-road routes and jeep trails connected to this road, and these trails also ran all the way south, eventually hitting the border.

Regular traffic ran on the road for the first few hours. Typically, our vehicle surveillance positions would see the vehicles approaching my location. They could then indicate whether or not I needed to pay attention as it came by my spot.

However, the southernmost vehicle position had a few blind spots north of their location, where four-wheel-drive dirt roads came out of the open desert and connected to the road I was sitting on. One of these dirt roads was a very popular, active smuggling route that hit the paved road just south of the Indian reservation boundary. These dirt-road connections were the spots I needed to be concerned about to ensure that a smuggler did not sneak out from a side route onto our main road without detection.

The good thing about this area was that it was almost completely dark and fairly remote. You could see for miles, and the secluded, open desert made hearing the slightest sounds easier. This was definitely advantageous for spotting or hearing the smugglers and allowed me to prepare for action.

It was past midnight. The night air had cooled off a few more degrees, and there hadn't been any traffic on the road for an hour. The sergeant had been doing routine check-ins with the team via the radio every hour just to make sure that everyone was not only okay but also awake. It was going to be a long night.

10.

SPIKING THE DOPE

AT ABOUT 1:30 A.M., the sergeant came over the radio to let us know that there was some activity on the smuggler radio network. I cannot go into the details on how he could hear this radio chatter, but it was great news. When the chatter picked up on the smuggler network, they had something moving through the routes.

Depending on which smugglers were talking on the radio, we could narrow down which area had movement because they all had assigned areas or duties. We knew we had dope moving our way, but we did not know precisely when or where it would show up. That changed in a moment, as our northern vehicle positions called out over the radio that a single vehicle was traveling on one of the close-by farm roads toward our main road.

This, by itself, was not too unusual because these farm fields had irrigators that would work through the night, making sure that fields got the water they needed. However, some of these irrigators worked two jobs out there. The first job was for the farm they irrigated, and the second was for the cartel. These workers were also quite good at keeping their cartel jobs under wraps. So, our surveillance positions kept an eye on this vehicle to see what it was up to while I kept my attention on the roads.

As the vehicle in question traveled closer to the main road, it stopped just before reaching the crossroad, which was the main road I was watching. It sat there for a few minutes, then pulled out onto the main road facing south, or the direction it had come from, and stopped. As I looked through my night vision, I could now see the headlights in the distance.

Within seconds, it turned off its headlights and went completely dark. The headlights then flashed back on and off again as they stayed parked on the road. Then the vehicle turned its headlights back on, made a quick U-turn to face back in the other direction, and stayed stationary with its lights on.

As I watched, I could hear the slight rumble of an engine to the south of my location. The engine got louder within seconds, sounding like the driver was pushing heavy on the gas. I then heard the unmistakable sound of a vehicle traveling over a cattle guard located south of me at the Indian reservation boundary.

The loud "fump fump" was a distinct signal that a vehicle had just crossed over the cattle guard, but I could not see any lights when I looked that way. A vehicle traveling on this road with no lights meant one thing, and by the time I would be able to see the vehicle, its occupants, and its cargo, it would be too late to try to spike the tires. I quickly prepared my spikes and got them in place on the road.

I then shifted my attention to the first vehicle, which now appeared to me to be what we call a "heat" vehicle. That is a car or truck the smugglers use to draw attention away from the vehicle loaded with drugs, or to make sure the route is clear for the loaded vehicle. The heat vehicle turned back onto the farm road it originally pulled out from and was sitting stationary with the lights on. It looked like it was waiting for the second vehicle to link up with it.

As I looked back south, I could now see the second vehicle I had only been able to hear to that point. I could not see it clearly, but I could tell it was a light-colored, full-size truck running without its lights. As it got closer, I could hear both the engine and the large, four-wheel-drive tires on the road.

I got on my radio to let my team know what was happening. The truck was traveling at a high rate of speed and quickly approached my position. I saw a single male driver. I could now make out that the truck was a quad-cab Chevrolet Avalanche, and I could also see that the cab was completely loaded with large bundles of marijuana.

I heard loud Mexican corridos from the speakers when the truck was about two hundred feet from my location. Within seconds, it was directly in front of me. Marijuana bundles also filled the entire bed of the truck, along with two spare four-wheel-drive tires resting on top of them.

The truck ran over the spikes, and I heard the gushing "woosh" associated with the rapid air loss from a tire. The sergeant listened to the driver get on his smuggler radio and yell, "Me pico!" He had figured out that he had been "spiked."

The driver punched it and headed toward the farm road where the heat vehicle waited. He braked hard but passed up the farm road slightly. He jammed the truck in reverse and began backing up. By then, all the tires had almost totally deflated, making the truck more difficult for the driver to operate and control.

The truck turned onto the farm road, and the heat vehicle that had been waiting took the lead. As they sped east, the sergeant had already called out on the radio for the vehicle teams to move in to intercept the smugglers.

Our people set up a perimeter and traveled parallel to the vehicles on nearby farm and dirt roads. The smuggler truck was losing its tires as they shredded from being driven on while flat. Chunks of the tires flew into the air, and the vehicle began to swerve back and forth, fishtailing as the driver started to lose control of the steering.

But the smugglers' vehicles still had a decent lead on our intercept vehicles. The damaged load truck went off-road into the desert and disappeared into some brush and mesquite tree thickets while the heat car continued at a high rate of speed on the farm road. Our team then had to pick which vehicle to keep following.

Knowing the load truck was full of dope, our team surrounded the area that it went into. They used night vision and moved slowly to ensure they did not miss the bad guy. Our vehicle teams got out on foot and began walking into the area where they last saw the truck.

Meanwhile, I got my gear together and prepared for my exfiltration. I had to gather everything and make my way back to my initial drop point on foot, as this was also my designated pickup location. Once I had all my gear, I began walking to the pickup location the same way I had come in, using my night vision and moving as stealthily as possible to ensure that I did not give away my position or the fact that I was in the area at all. I monitored the radio traffic of the rest of my team the entire time to stay updated on the chase.

The teams tracking the truck had picked up the tracks traveling across the open desert and were now moving in on the brush and tree cluster. As they approached the tree line, they could hear the music from the truck and used that to pinpoint it within the thicket. Within minutes, they had located the truck.

It was in a small wash hidden within the thicket and had stopped after getting stuck on a dirt berm. The driver's door was wide open, and the radio and engine were still on. Our team moved in, cleared the truck for any occupants, and began looking for shoe prints from the bad guy who had fled.

The truck was completely loaded with bundles of

marijuana, which, after processing, ended up weighing just over 1,500 pounds. All of the interior seats except the driver's seat had been removed to pack the cab with as much marijuana as possible.

There were the remnants of snack foods consumed by the driver on his overnight trip from Mexico. There were also a few narco trinkets, such as a Jesus Malverde card and a small Santa Muerte ornament. Again, smugglers and cartel members often carried these narco trinkets, believing these "saints" would bring them protection and safe passage.

It was still dark. Our team was unsure of the driver's location and didn't know if there were cartel ground scouts in the area. They brought their vehicles closer to the truck and turned all the lights on—including the red-and-blues. We always wanted to be sure that any smugglers in the area knew that we were law enforcement rather than a rival group or rip crew.

Once everyone was by the load vehicle, our team set up a protective perimeter to avoid any cartel members from coming in to attempt to take their load back. As you can imagine, losing a load of this size would have ramifications for everyone involved on the cartel side. Some of these members would be more than willing to go toe-to-toe with law enforcement if it meant getting their load back and not facing cartel discipline.

There were also scouts and cartel members in that area who were referred to as "punteros," which roughly translates to "leading." These cartel members held responsibility for the load when it was in their area. They would not hesitate to deploy their local "soldados," or soldiers, to do the job. This is what made our scene a little more dangerous.

When I arrived at my "exfil" location, my ride was already waiting for me. I quickly loaded my gear and jumped in as we slowly crept out of that area and back to the truck's location.

I asked my partner if we were "on sign," which meant I was asking if our people had located and were following the footprints of the bad guy. My partner said we had located a "foot sign," which was a shoe track of some type. However, we did not have the resources to follow them at that particular time. It would be too easy for the bad guy to use that to divide us and attempt to take the load back. So, in this case, we needed to remain with the load and secure it while we waited for more backup to arrive.

The sergeant called for backup, and a couple of marked patrol units made their way to our location. We now had a pretty solid security team, so we just waited until our evidence tow truck arrived to load and take possession of the truck. By this time, the morning sun had started to show its face on the eastern horizon of the desert.

I will always remember the awesome Arizona sunrise from working these smuggling routes and operations. Just before dawn, before the sun showed itself, the horizon would start to get light, and any clouds in the eastern sky would light up with bright oranges, reds, pinks, and purples as the rays of the coming sunshine would blast through them toward the heavens.

There would be a distinct calmness in the desert during this time, and the morning would be cool. A small amount of moisture would amplify the unique smell of moist palo verde trees and greasewood brush that was so unique to our southwest desert. You could not help but get lost in that for a moment. It was a tangible reminder of what a great God there was to create such a beautiful scene. Shortly after sunrise, the tow truck arrived to take the load truck to our evidence yard at our main station.

The sergeant had to make one last plan in order to bring this operation to a close for the night. He needed to make a security plan for at least one of the vehicle teams to provide security for the tow truck as it transported the load truck. During this last transport, there was still a risk that the cartel would try to recover their lost load, so we had to ensure that we had security to counter them if they did.

The sergeant selected the security team, and they departed with the tow truck to the main station. The rest of us headed to our briefing location before going home for the day. We completed the debrief and put all the equipment away. Then we headed home to get some sleep.

This thirty- to forty-five-minute drive was often the hardest part of the day. I would have to fight to stay alert and awake on the drive home after an excitement-filled night with plenty of adrenaline dumps.

Once I made it home, I had the opportunity to spend a little time with my family as they were getting ready for school and work. Once they were off to their day, it was time to hit the sack and recharge for the next night.

11.

THE DEVIL IS IN THE DETAILS

A S I MOVED INTO MY NEW POSITION as the narcotics sergeant, the smuggling corridor had been very active. The cartels were literally moving tons of dope through the smuggling routes in our county. We had recruited some pretty good sources who were either directly involved or worked on the periphery with the cartels.

These sources provided some pretty insightful and helpful intelligence that our crew could take action on. We learned everything from the names of specific people involved and their job within the cartel to factual information on when and where a drug load would be coming through. The information allowed us to constantly move on to new investigations and do a lot of work in the desert going after the large smuggling drug loads.

At this point in my career, I had moved through the different jobs associated with these desert operations. I understood how each piece of the overall operation was meant to function. Now, as the new sergeant over narcotics, I was making the calls and planning the operations. The outgoing sergeant was riding with me for one of his last operations to help me out and, quite frankly, get in a few reps before moving on to his next assignment.

Like any operation, we met at our designated spot to brief, give out assignments, and get started for the night. When we finished, the sergeant jumped in my assigned truck with me, and we headed out for the night. We were in a rootbeer-brown, quad-cab Ford F-150. It even had custom desert pinstriping—consisting of small scratches down both sides of the truck from running it through the brush in these desert operations.

We loaded up our gear and snacks, stopped to gas up, and headed toward the area where we would work. It had rained earlier, and it was a warm night, so the air was a little more humid and sticky than our normal dry-heat air.

We were designated as a surveillance-and-chase vehicle for any bad-guy rides that came across our path. I had to be on my game for driving. My copilot had to be on his game to communicate on the radio and be my lookout for ambushes or other dangers that might pop up during these chases.

As we approached the area where we would be work-ing, it was time for us to disappear by going dark ("black-ing out"). From this point forward, we would be running without lights to get into our assigned area without the cartel scouts detecting us and advising all the other bad guys of our presence.

When I prepared to do this, I would always go through a checklist of sorts. I ensured that my night vision was turned on, that I got the visual feedback showing me they were on by the slight green glow that came from the eye-pieces, and that I heard the positive click when they locked into my head mount (a.k.a. my skull crusher). However, in my excitement to get started, I slightly overlooked one crucial piece that would teach me an important lesson of following every step.

I had turned on my night-vision goggles and could see the infamous green glow coming from the eyepieces, so I knew that they were on and functioning. I then moved to mount them onto my head mount. I got the click I was looking for as they locked in the up position, meaning that they were still sitting above my eyes, and I had not yet pulled them down. I then checked with my partner to ensure that he was also prepared. He had followed these same steps in prepping his gear and gave me the affirmative that he was good to go.

Now it was "go-time," and that meant lights out. I lowered my night-vision goggles, reached down to turn off my headlights, and flipped on my kill switch, which turned off my running and brake lights. As my truck went completely dark under the dark and overcast desert sky, I quickly found that I could see dark green but nothing else … no objects, no outlines, nothing.

I went into stress mode and worked to figure out what was going on. When you have that stress and adrenaline dump, you revert back to training and experience in situations like this. The only problem, in this case, was that I did not have a file to go to for this type of problem. I adjusted my gain on the night-vision goggles to increase their brightness, but it didn't work.

As I drove down the main highway at approximately sixty-five miles per hour, I still could not see where I was going. Unbeknownst to me, my attempt to fix the problem was causing me to drift slightly to the right side of the highway. I continued to work on the issue while my truck continued to drift to the right at high speed. I started to panic slightly. By now, my partner had figured out that something was not right.

I felt the ever-familiar vibration hum of the rumble strip. It told me I was starting to drift onto the shoulder of the road. When you work the night shift—which I did for most of my career—you become very familiar with the rumble strip. It had saved my life many times when I was on my way home from a long overnight shift, simply by waking me as I started to doze off and drift a little. We jokingly referred to the rumble strip as driving by braille, and anyone who has worked the graveyard shift has likely had this same experience.

I also knew that this road had an approximate thirty-five-degree downward slope to the shoulder. I abandoned my night-vision goggles, ripping them off and turning on my headlights as I began to travel further onto the right shoulder. I let off the gas as my truck started to lean right because of the slope.

As my headlights came back on, my passenger and I saw that I was not only almost entirely on the dirt portion of the shoulder of the roadway, but I was headed straight for a large wooden power pole. My training kicked in, and I gave my steering wheel some slight input to bring me back to the left and onto the asphalt. The rear of my truck started to fishtail slightly, but I gave the steering wheel a little input and brought it under control as we whipped back up onto the road.

By this time, my partner was simply along for the ride and was in a bit of a panic because he had no control of the wild ride I had just taken us on. I had literally almost killed us. As he gained his composure, he yelled loudly, "Miklo, what the fuck are you doing?!"

I nervously laughed as I slowed down to a stop and regained my composure. The adrenaline dump made my heart beat like I had just run an Olympic sprint, and I worked to control my breathing to bring my heart rate back down. I sheepishly explained to my partner that I could not see through my night-vision goggles when I put them on, so I was basically going down the road at sixty-five miles per hour, totally blind.

As I rolled to a stop, I pulled over to figure out what was going on and, quite frankly, to get out and walk around for a minute to get my heart rate back down. I turned on the truck's interior light and quickly found the issue: I had forgotten to remove the protective lens covers from my night-vision goggles.

These covers are designed to protect the tubes from

being exposed to bright light that could ruin the goggles, so they allow you to see through the night-vision goggles but filter out almost all ambient light. Translation: in low-light darkness, you ain't seeing much!

This small mistake had almost proven catastrophic for me that night, and it's just one example of how much paying attention to detail mattered in each and every mission. It also serves as an example of how we learned our craft. We didn't have a manual or training course for these types of operations, and most of the time, we were learning on the fly and making it up as we went.

With my slight but huge error now corrected and my equipment back in order, I took a deep breath, killed all of my lights again, and started heading into our staging location for the night. We would take our time when we worked our way into these spots because we understood that there were cartel lookouts everywhere, so we had to mind how noisy and visible we were.

Sometimes, even the glint of the moon reflecting off our windshield or the crunching of gravel under our tires could give away our position. So we would drive very carefully, with our windows down, to ensure that we could see and hear as much as possible. We would even stop to check our surroundings occasionally and listen for anything out of the ordinary or suspicious. At night, the open desert can carry sounds much further than you realize. This would prove very true tonight.

We slowly gained ground as we headed toward our final spot, taking in the ever-present smell of the greasewood brush, the sounds of mooing cows, and the scream of bullfrogs in the ponds that irrigated the farm fields. We eventually made it to our staging location. I positioned my vehicle in some trees to give me additional cover to hide any shiny features my truck might have under the moonlight.

We would often put some extra covering on our vehicles, which was called "brushing up." We would take tree branches and even camouflage tarps and place them over the vehicle to hide it as much as possible.

The cartels knew their area and what to look for. We were playing a cat-and-mouse game, and the only way to beat them at their own game was to use their methods against them. I finished brushing up my truck, and with all the windows down, I turned off my engine. Then it became a sit-and-wait game.

We were working off of some pretty reliable intelligence that told us the cartel would be moving some loads by vehicle tonight. However, we only had the last-known location of the load vehicle, which was just north of the Mexico border. That meant that the vehicle (or vehicles) could show up in our area anytime from a couple of hours to early the next morning. Without more accurate intelligence, we would have to lie in wait and hope that they showed up sooner rather than later.

As we sat in the truck talking, we could hear the desert come alive with all the sounds of an Arizona night. In the distance, the howls of a coyote pack rang through the night, which can almost sound like someone crying. We would hear the occasional owl and, of course, the open-range cattle moving through. The pests would also show up, and the buzz and whine of mosquitos dive-bombing our ears almost drove us insane at times.

As we chatted during this quiet time, I thought I could hear a low rumble. I couldn't quite make out what it was, but it kind of sounded like a far-off train approaching. You know that low rumble that you kind of hear and feel at the same time? It's the sound of train cars as they rumble across the tracks in the distance. The only problem was that we didn't have any train tracks nearby, so the sound was out of the ordinary.

My partner heard the same thing and asked me what the hell it was. I listened more intently. I told him I could hear it, but I couldn't quite make out what it was. As we sat still and listened closely, it sounded like the rumble would go lower and then higher. Then it hit both of us—it was an engine.

In the open desert, we could often hear the low roar of an engine—especially that of a truck or an SUV—for miles before it got to us. Once we became familiar with the sound, we had a better gauge to tell what it was the next time we heard it. There was no doubt. We could both hear it, and we knew it was damn close.

The only problem was that we could not tell which direction it was coming from, and there were no head-lights or anything to accompany the sound of the engine. We were both on high alert because any vehicle traveling without lights in this area meant only one thing: smug-glers.

Within minutes, our suspicions were confirmed when we saw a four-wheel-drive truck crest over a canal bank. It was about one hundred yards in front of us on the other side of the asphalt road. There was almost a full moon, and the clouds had moved out for the most part. We could see the truck clearly, as every shiny part of the truck lit up and glowed under the moonlight, even without any lights on.

We hastily geared up to go. I turned the keys in the

ignition and fired up my truck. The sound of my truck starting was covered by the loud exhaust of the quickly-approaching vehicle. I fully anticipated it to turn onto the paved road in front of us and figured I would follow behind, blacked out, driving with my night vision on.

This was one of my proven tactics—to follow the vehicle at a slight distance without them knowing we were even there. However, it was a learned art because I had to stay close enough to keep an eye on the vehicle but not so close that its brake lights would give my position away when they would slow or stop to make turns.

But my plan instantly changed as the truck shot straight across the road, almost coming at us head-on, and blew right past us at about forty-five miles per hour. It happened so fast that it caught me off guard. Your mind reacting to a problem in front of you is always behind the curve, especially when you anticipate one thing happening and something totally different happens at the last moment.

The driver had obviously noticed us at that point and had punched it as he passed our position, heading straight into the open desert behind us. As my brain processed what was taking place, I floored the gas pedal and cranked my steering wheel, starting a tire-spinning donut until my truck faced the same direction the smuggler had gone.

I straightened out my steering wheel and floored the gas pedal again as I traveled onto the small four-wheel-drive road the truck was on. The bad guys now had a good half-mile head start on us. I could see their brake lights activate and bounce up and down as they traveled over the rough desert terrain.

My partner jumped on the radio to let the other units know what was happening, as this truck had crept past all the other positions and somehow snuck right up on us. We were now in a full-on car chase. The bad guys were gaining ground on us and getting away. The truck still had its lights off, but we could see the brake lights activate occasionally and bounce up and down as they continued further into the desert and the territory they controlled.

The decision was swiftly made to abort this chase because we felt that we could be getting drawn into an ambush at worst and, at best, could completely compromise all of our resources and positions to catch a stolen vehicle. So, I slowly came to a stop. We regained our bearings and made sure we had not fallen into any type of ambush.

I worked my way back to our starting position, where the truck had initially passed us. We got out and conducted a quick check of the area on foot. We wanted to make damn sure that bad guys had not slipped into the area during the chaos of the chase we were just involved in. A quick check gave us the peace of mind that the vicinity was still free of bad guys, and we jumped back in the truck.

We were not sure if we had compromised our mission for the night and if this short interruption had given our position and our team's position away. We sat for the next several hours with absolutely no activity other than the creatures and animals of the desert in their nightly rituals of hunting or gathering food and scurrying around the desert floors.

That night, we talked about everything from family, to cases we were working, to current events, and we noticed every so often just how dull the night had become. We hoped this was simply a lull and that the cartels had not aborted operations in this area for the night.

Close to dawn, we recognized that it was time for us to start moving out of the area. We would need to sneak out of our hiding locations the same way we snuck in to ensure that we did not give away our position to the many scouts who would be up and watching when the sun broke along the horizon, bringing the desert day to life. We eventually moved toward a predetermined location where we would meet the rest of our crew to discuss what had happened during that night and make plans for the next operation.

We met at a spot a little east of where our operation had taken place but still within the vicinity of the smuggling routes, as the farm roads that ran west to east from the smuggling corridor also ran directly into an area filled with cartel stash houses. There was a nice spot that was somewhat hidden by several trees and brush lines, and it was slightly lower in elevation than the farm roads. We often used this meeting location because it gave us enough cover to park our vehicles and gather around to talk.

The crew started off with the standard smack-talking and joking. I excused myself to walk off toward the brush line to relieve myself from the considerable amount of caffeinated drinks I had steadily drunk all night to stay awake and alert.

As I was making my way toward the brush, I maintained a high level of awareness because we were still in an area active with smugglers. I carefully made my way toward the trees, and as I did, I saw what I thought was a Hispanic male pop up and duck back down behind the lower brush next to the tree line.

It appeared that this guy was unaware that I was approaching. He was looking away from me, toward the west. My mind began to race; I thought he looked like a ground scout. I could've sworn that I saw a radio in his hand. The cartel used scouts all along the smuggling routes to serve as lookouts.

However, I was also exhausted by this time, and part of me wondered if my mind was playing tricks on me—maybe I am just imagining things. Despite the internal argument about what I thought I saw, I knew that I had to check it out to verify. I methodically moved toward the location where I believed I saw the scout, ensuring that I was quiet and slow-moving so I wouldn't spook him.

As I approached the brush line, I slowly gained elevation and started to see more of the farm fields to the north and west of our current location. As I slowed down even more, minding each step as if I were hunting my prey for a close-proximity pouncing, a distant noise redirected my attention.

I heard what sounded like a low-flying jet plane approaching from a distance. This sound confused me, as this particular area was not in the flight path for any airports or even the military. Tired and now perplexed by hearing what I thought was an approaching jet, I began scanning the horizon in all directions.

As I looked west, I immediately noticed a large dirt cloud emerging down the same farm road I was now standing next to. If you have ever seen race cars going for land speed records out on huge, dry lake beds and the trail of dust they leave behind, it looked exactly like that.

I scanned forward on the dirt trail to catch up to whatever was making that trail and creating the jet-like sound. I saw two trucks that looked like Ford F-150 quad-cabs traveling at a high rate of speed and coming straight toward me. The trucks were still approximately one mile away, but at the speed they were traveling, they would be on top of me in no time.

I had an immediate adrenaline dump as my mind registered what I was seeing and hearing. These two trucks were load vehicles, meaning they were loaded with drugs. Depending on how well they packed them, these trucks were typically loaded with anywhere from 1,500 to 2,000 pounds of marijuana. While this was not normal for them to travel after daybreak, there was no doubt about who they were. And that they were coming my way.

Once this had registered in my brain, I turned and sprinted back toward my guys and our vehicles. I was about a hundred yards away when I began yelling, "Load trucks!" as I waved my hands over my head in hopes that it would alarm everyone into getting to their vehicles quickly.

It had the desired effect, and as I got to my truck, my partner was already inside on the passenger side and had started it up for me. I floored the gas and cranked the wheel to spin out and rotate to change my direction. The truck did exactly what I wanted it to, and I quickly faced the direction I needed to head—straight toward the cut-off point for the two approaching trucks. In the meantime, one of my other guys had made his way to a farm road further east of us and moved north in an attempt to box the trucks in.

I approached the intersection where they would cross, and they both shot across the farm road in front of me, traveling together in tandem with about half a car length between them. Just as I thought, they were two Ford F-150s fully loaded with marijuana packs.

There was a single occupant in each truck. Both of them were young-looking Hispanic males. One truck was red (I'll call this the red load truck), and the other (I'll call it the brown load truck) was the exact same color as the F-150 I was driving.

They basically dusted us out when they blew by in front of us. As I turned behind them, I quickly lost sight of both trucks. When the dust settled, I could see they had significantly slowed down after realizing that more of my team members were approaching them from the other direction, essentially cutting them off.

The farm road we were on was pretty dry, but it was between two cotton fields that had been recently irrigated and were both very wet and muddy. The trucks were somewhat trapped between us.

As our team cut off their route, the red load truck began to do donuts between my vehicle and my team on the other side. The driver was doing this to create a smokescreen using the powdery farm dust. He was trying to cause some confusion. The brown load truck began to do the same, and then they quickly separated.

The red load truck traveled back in my direction. The brown load truck drove toward my other team. It moved slightly into one of the fields without sinking completely to the axles and managed to squeeze around our guys blocking the road.

Our guys turned their vehicles around and chased the brown load truck, traveling approximately seventy to eighty miles per hour on the dirt farm road. The smugglers were heading toward a small cartel neighborhood about four miles away, doing their best to get to what they considered a safe zone. This neighborhood had many cartel stash houses where they could run to and hide.

Meanwhile, I dealt with the red load truck. The large dust cloud formed by the two vehicles had begun to settle and clear. I could now see through the dust that the red load truck was closing the distance between us. I slowed to almost a stop, preparing for the driver's next move. There were really only two options: he was going to ram us, or he was going to drive around us.

To my surprise, he also began to slow, and it appeared that he was moving to his right in an attempt to pass us on the driver's side of my truck. As he passed me on my side, we both had a very clear view of each other. Our driver's side windows aligned, and we were face-to-face. We locked eyes—his head and eyes tracked on mine while we passed each other. In the young man's face, I could see what appeared to be extreme confusion.

I let out an audible laugh as I suddenly figured out why he looked so confused when staring me in the face. In the confusion of the dust cloud, the vehicles got mixed up, and the driver of the red load truck lost track of the brown load truck. As he traveled toward my vehicle and slowed, the driver thought he was approaching the brown load truck since it looked exactly like mine. The driver of the red load truck was trying to figure out how a long-haired white guy had taken control of their load vehicle.

Still chuckling at how confused the driver of the red load truck looked, I cranked the steering wheel hard to the left and simultaneously stomped on the gas pedal to spin my vehicle around and give chase. The technique was one of my favorite moves to turn in the opposite direction quickly, and it worked like a champ once again.

I chased the red load truck as he sped up and continued back to the west, where the two vehicles had come from. We were traveling on the same dirt farm road I had first seen them on, and we were hauling ass.

My crew split up. Some members went after the brown F150, while the other part of the crew jumped in with me to chase the red truck. It had a good lead and was at least a half-mile ahead of us. I gave it everything I had to try to gain ground on him. He shot across the last paved road that ran north and south and continued on the other side to a four-wheel-drive road that went directly into the desert.

Driving got tricky because the road would drop into a small wash, follow the wash for a bit, pop back out into the open desert, and wind around mesquite tree clusters, greasewood bushes, and saguaro cactus. The desert looks wide open from the air, but when you are on the desert floor, it is thicker than you realize with all of the plant life.

Couple this with the driver's damn good driving skills, and within minutes, I had lost sight of him.

Once that happened, we had to track the vehicle using the same techniques we used on backpackers. It's very much like how a hunter tracks his prey. With the terrain switching between hard and soft ground, you would be surprised at how hard it can be to stay on the track of a vehicle if that is all you are working with. Combine this with the fact that any cartel scouts in the area would now be on high alert and providing guidance to the load driver via their radio system, and the bad guys could disappear quickly.

Within minutes, I realized that we had lost the red load truck. I let the rest of my team know what had happened via our radio. We then slowed down, backtracked, and tried to relocate tracks we may have missed.

We often turned off our vehicles and listened to pick up the sound of the fleeing vehicle in the open desert. It would brake and accelerate hard, and the rough road would rattle every piece of metal on that truck. So we employed every tactic and technique we knew to get back on its track.

A few minutes later, one of the other team members came over the radio and excitedly told us they had located the truck, wrecked and abandoned. That team member gave some quick directions and landmarks, and we made our way to the location. When we got close, we started to see tire tracks and vegetation that had been run over, allowing us to follow these tracks to the vehicle's final resting spot.

We saw our team and the red load truck stuck in front of us. The driver had run it into a small cluster of mesquite trees in an attempt to hide it. When he did this, the truck's undercarriage became stuck on a high spot of dirt. This, in turn, elevated the tires off of the ground. The truck couldn't move. The driver ran, but he had taken the few-minutes-headstart that he had to try to cover the top and bed of the vehicle with some loose brush and tree branches to camouflage it further.

The driver's efforts to get away had worked for him. But fortunately for us, we were able to secure his loaded truck carrying approximately 1,500 pounds of raw, Mexican-grown, harvested, and packaged marijuana with a street value (at that time) of about $750,000.

As we secured the vehicle and the surrounding area to ensure our driver was not hiding nearby, we got word from the other half of our team. They were on their way to our location after losing the brown load truck.

When traveling on the dirt back roads and through farm fields, the dirt often became so soft that it created a very thick dust cloud, ensuring we had zero visibility. This is what had happened to our guys chasing the brown load truck. Visibility had become so bad in a few spots that they had to come to complete stops to let the dust settle enough to be able to drive through it.

Each time this happened, the brown load truck gained more and more ground on them. As the driver continued east toward the stash house neighborhoods, our guys were at least a mile behind him. This gave the driver enough lead to reach the neighborhood and disappear into the garage of a stash house where they were awaiting his arrival.

What began as a slow night and ended as an adrenaline-pumping day turned out to be a success. While one of the load trucks had gotten away, along with a stolen truck from earlier in the night, we had still captured one stolen load truck and the dope it contained. This, and the intelligence we got from things left behind in the truck, made it a huge success in our world.

Being successful in some form or fashion was always a plus to help keep us motivated in this game.

Matt with a confiscated load of drugs seized from the cartels after a chase through the desert.

Bulk marijuana backpacks seized after a group of backpackers were taken into custody in Pinal County.

12.

SHOOTOUT IN THE DESERT

IT WAS SPRING OF 2010. The Sinaloa cartel fully controlled the smuggling into and through our county. Pinal County was in the limelight because of the hot, political topic of immigration. President Barack Obama's policies had fueled the fire for the cartel's chokehold on the smuggling routes into the U.S., and specifically, into our county.

Vekol Valley was a large valley area just south of Interstate 8 on the Pinal County and Maricopa County line, in the most southwestern part of Pinal County. This valley was entirely controlled by the cartel out of the Mexican state of Sinaloa, the Cártel de Sinaloa or CDS. It was headed by the infamous Joaquin "El Chapo" Guzman.

The Sinaloa cartel controlled this landscape like a well-organized military unit, with scouts on the hilltops from the Mexico-United States border all the way to just south of the Phoenix Metro area. These scouts held key overwatch positions for the numerous hiking trails, dirt roads, and four-wheel-drive trails that ran throughout the open desert leading up to Interstate 8 from Mexico.

The cartel had security elements ready to defend any of the territories these scouts were responsible for because there were rip crews who regularly roamed the areas and conducted their violent robberies on unsuspecting trans- porters for the cartel.

This spring afternoon, Vekol Valley was about to be thrust into the local and national headlines as it would become the scene of an officer-involved shooting. That fact alone usually drew a large amount of police and me- dia activity, but this shooting would have the added piece of cartel involvement. This, of course, made it "sexy" for all those news outlets, as they could spin it into political agendas.

At this time, I had moved back to the Traffic Unit as a uniformed sergeant and worked on a motorcycle as part of these duties. (I was also on the SWAT team, which was part-time and only when we were activated). On this day, I was in uniform and had already worked a few accidents and some speed enforcement. I was in our main office in Florence catching up on paperwork when the call came over the air: "998/999," which are codes for an "officer-involved shooting" and "officer needs emergency assistance."

I heard a few of these calls come over the radio in my career, and they send a chill up my spine every time. There is no way to prepare for the call or stop the emotions that flood your mind and body when you hear it.

I listened closely to the radio as the dispatcher provided further information on the deputy involved, the situation, and the location. As I listened to the broadcast, the report got worse. They did not have a location on the deputy involved in the shooting, other than he was in the Vekol Valley area on a hiking trail and had been shot.

Dispatch was frantically working to narrow down the location of the deputy who had called in on his cell phone because the reception for our police radios was horrible in that area.

The good news was that the deputy was talking and trying to give them as much information as possible. The bad news was that they still did not have an exact location on him, and the deputy said he had been engaged in a gunfight by multiple bad guys. They had him surrounded and had the high ground, and they were exchanging gunfire.

The investigation would later reveal that our deputy had stumbled into a rip crew who had taken a load of drugs from a group of cartel backpackers. The deputy had seen the men while checking the area and began tracking them himself. This was not protocol, but this particular deputy was a little hardheaded like that, and he had now gotten himself in deeper than he had anticipated.

In this instance, the rip crew had set him up, leading him into a small area where they'd set up an ambush. They jumped up and opened fire when he reached the ambush point. The deputy was taken by surprise but was able to get to a large rock for cover just after being grazed in his side by a bullet. Although he was able to return fire on at least a couple of the bad guys he could see, there was a problem. They had secured the high ground and outnumbered him. That's when he called our dispatch center via the 911 system.

As our deputy did his best to hold his own, cops started to head toward his general location. There is one thing that always goes well in a situation like this—every cop within driving distance will come together quickly to assist their fellow cop. The same was true in this case.

There were cops from about a one-hundred-mile radius screaming down streets and highways to get to our deputy. Nobody cared who he worked for, who he was, or the circumstances. We all just knew that we had another cop in dire need of assistance against some of the worst bad guys out there, and we were going to help.

Switching to my role on the SWAT team, I raced toward my motorcycle parked in our lot, running alongside several other SWAT team members headed to their vehicles. I was still wearing my police uniform, and the one advantage I had to get there quickly was my motorcycle. It allowed me to maneuver through traffic at higher speeds and get through areas much quicker than a regular car.

The disadvantage was that I was in my motor outfit, which consisted of high boots and breeches. I also had zero extra gear for a desert operation. But I didn't care at that point and just wanted to get out there to help our guy.

On my way, I could hear a flood of radio traffic through our dispatch from all of the different responding units. There was still one huge problem—we did not have an exact location of the deputy. He had parked his vehicle in one area and then hiked into the hills, where he started tracking the bad guys. But we knew the general area and air assets were heading that way. Once in the area, the helicopters could cover a lot of ground to pinpoint his location.

It took me about thirty minutes to get to the location designated as the incident rally area, known as the "double gates" on the south side of Interstate 8, right at the Pinal County and Maricopa County line. This area was where our guy had parked and got out on foot. It was now where about thirty cops from eight to ten different agencies gathered.

As I parked my motorcycle, I recognized a detective with his rifle and made my way over to him to see if he had any updated information. He said that all he knew was that the Highway Patrol helicopter was in the air, and they thought they knew what area our guy was in but had not found him yet. I asked him if he happened to have an extra rifle. He didn't but quickly took off his rifle and gave it to me.

I then saw my step-cousin, who was a SWAT member for the Arizona Highway Patrol. I asked him if he had any extra pants and boots. He did, and by some crazy miracle, they were my size. I quickly changed my pants and boots as more officers and resources arrived. It was starting to look like the major incident that it was, with local, state, and federal cops all on the scene.

Once I changed into more appropriate gear for the desert, a few other SWAT team members showed up. We got word that two helicopters were in the air, one from the Maricopa County Sheriff's Office and the other from the Highway Patrol. They had located our guy near the shootout scene and were bringing him back to our location, where an ambulance and medical personnel were standing by. A few minutes later, both helicopters were on the ground at our site, and our guy was loaded into the ambulance.

I now had a small element of my SWAT guys dressed and ready to go, so I checked in at the ad hoc command post on the trunk of a patrol car and let them know that my team would head into the shooting location to secure it.

I made my way over to the gurney and asked our guy how he was doing. He was admittedly in some pain but said he was good. I did a quick rundown, debriefing with him and trying to get as much information as possible— any details about the bad guys and the site of the shooting. He did not have much for me on their descriptions other than believing they were either dark-complected Hispanics or Native Americans. He also gave me the clothing description of the main guy in the shootout.

With that information, I ran over to the Maricopa County helicopter, which was large enough to take my team of three SWAT members and myself into the area where the shooting occurred. As we boarded the aircraft, I asked the pilot about our live weapons and some small explosive devices on our gear because I knew these were not usually allowed. The pilot told me that we were fine. We had to be ready for a gunfight, so the standard protocols were not in place.

My team and I buckled in and jumped on the helicopter communications. We were in the air within seconds, and the pilot asked where we wanted him to drop us. If the pilot had spotted any bad guys, we wanted to get dropped in right on top of them. But the pilot indicated they had not seen any other people in the area when they located our guy and got him out. I told him to take us back to where they had picked our guy up, so we could secure that area.

We began to circle a small valley. The pilot told me they had forgotten to mark the exact coordinates of where they had found our guy, and they were now trying to find the spot. We continued to orbit the small valley, and the pilot said he believed that this was the valley but that he did not know the location of where our guy had been. I needed to make a quick tactical decision. We were looking for a needle in a haystack.

I knew that the bad guys would do one of two things—stay put in that area and hide really well, or haul ass south to try to get as far away as possible from the crime scene. My gut told me that option two was the most likely option, so I told the pilot to head south to the next mountaintop and drop us there.

This would put us on top of a small but fairly steep and high hill about a mile south of the shooting location. Landing there would give us the high ground. We could counter any ambush or attack better while we used binoculars to "glass" the valleys around the hill to locate our bad guys.

The pilot got us to the top of the hill and gently touched the skids on the ground, and we jumped off the helicopter as they hovered. We took up positions that we had practiced many times, kneeling under the hovering helicopter and providing outward cover with our rifles as they lifted off. The aircraft slowly became smaller and smaller as it returned to the command post to grab more of our SWAT guys.

My team and I gathered up and checked each other to ensure everyone was good to go. Once we had done that, I saw a good rock ledge a couple of hundred yards away and decided that would be our stronghold. We tactically moved toward the rocks, not knowing if the bad guys were close by and ready for us.

We cleared our way forward and into the rock ledge. We found it unoccupied and a good spot for both cover behind large rocks and overlooking the valleys below. We quickly set up security, with a couple of guys watching our back while two of us searched the surrounding areas below us for any signs of movement or people.

I would later find out that, as this was happening, the United States Border Patrol had begun to set up a large perimeter of this entire vicinity. It was approximately one hundred square miles, with agents lining any travel routes, roads, or trails in or out of the area. Additionally, the FBI and an element of the NSA had arrived on the scene. They tried to use some of their intelligence gathering and monitoring technology to locate the bad guys.

This entire operation and the personnel involved ended up being one of the largest and most impressive operations I have seen in my career. The sheer number of agencies involved, the assets and technology they brought, the willingness to assist us in any way, and the hours they put in over the next day or so were amazing, to say the least.

As all of that took place, a second, small element of my SWAT team members loaded onto a helicopter and flew into our area. We could see the helicopter just before it descended into a valley out of our sight. Apparently, they had pinpointed the location of the shooting, or at least the spot where they picked up our injured guy. They dropped our second team there.

We had good radio communications with the second team both in the air and on the ground. However, we found that we had lost contact with our command post. So, our second team acted as a relay for us, relaying any necessary information from the command post to our team and back.

By now, it was late afternoon, and we had been in our position for a couple of hours. Honestly, I had anticipated that the bad guys would be looking for a fight and that we would be engaged with them sooner rather than later. I had thought we might be done just before dark, but now it looked like we would be out here most of the night. We were losing some of our advantages because of our hasty deployment. We were dressed in hotter-weather gear and had not brought our night-vision equipment.

As I started to focus on my team's well-being, I had a distinct feeling that we were being watched and maybe even maneuvered on. I had no solid evidence of this—just that weird "Spidey sense" that had saved my bacon on more than one occasion. So I made a quick tactical decision to start a fight with any remaining cartel members trying to maneuver on us or hunkering down and hiding to wait us out.

With all this information running through my head, I did the only thing that came to mind in that instance. I told my guys to take a good position of cover for fighting and stand by. As the guys got into place, I climbed onto a large boulder at the edge of the mountaintop. It was essentially a sheer cliff looking down over the valley below us.

Keep in mind that I was a little fired up because they had shot one of our people, and I was trying to start a fight. I knew that Mexican men are very proud and hold their mothers in a very special place of reverence. Most of us hold our mothers in a special place, but the Mexican culture is at a whole different level. I also knew that every man had an ego, and cartel and gang members especially had a reputation to uphold.

So I went a little colorful on the language, which I have been known to do from time to time. As I stood and looked over the valley with my rifle at the low-ready, I screamed at the top of my lungs into the valley below, "Chinga tu pinche madres, hijos de putas! Levantate como los hombres pinche putos!" Loosely translated in street slang that I grew up hearing: "Fuck your fucking mothers, you sons of bitches! Get up like fucking men, you bitches!"

I figured that one of two things would happen if true cartel "soldados" were hiding around us. Either my challenge would elicit a violent response and choice words back at me about my mother, my heritage and family, and well-wishes for my immediate death, or it would remain quiet because there were no fighters in the area.

To my dismay, there were no shots headed our way and no screaming back at me in Spanish. The valley remained calm and quiet.

I waited a few minutes and let my barrage of insults settle in, just in case I had a bad guy trying to decide if he would let it slide or not. After several minutes of silence, I repeated my challenge and used some street-slang Spanish to question their manhood, sexuality, and worth. Again, I got no response and realized that either my tactics were not working or the cartel members had indeed vacated the valley.

Recognizing that this operation would not be over anytime soon, I focused on the fact that we were dangerously low on water. This time of year was shorts-and-t-shirt weather during the day, and we would need pants and a light coat at night.

As dusk approached, it started to cool off, and our gear—soaked in sweat from both heat and pumping adrenaline—was getting colder by the minute. With the temperature drop and a light breeze, a few of us started to shiver slightly. We all knew that being dehydrated and cold was not a good combination.

We hadn't seen any movement, and our technology didn't show any activity in our area. Our second team had located the crime scene and secured it as best they could to preserve what remained of it. They had also set themselves up to defend it and themselves in case the bad guys had stayed in that area and made a run at their team.

We tightened our team inside the rock ledge and prepared for darkness to settle in. We got routine check-ins from the command post and had to relay our check-ins through our second team. We had also notified the command post that we needed water as soon as possible. They were already planning to deliver water to our location using the helicopters.

We sat on the mountaintop as darkness fell. We began operating on our hearing and used white light if we needed to check anything. Using white light was problematic because it didn't illuminate much, and you would instantly give your position away to any bad guys in the area. So, we chose to stay dark for the tactical advantage unless it was absolutely necessary to use our light.

Sitting in the dark, we figured out where we were relative to our second team as the helicopter delivered the first load of water to them. We were actually about a mile further south of the second team than we initially thought.

We could see the helicopter break out of its hover over our second team and head our way. We had been out of water for a couple of hours by this time. We were, without a doubt, dehydrated and feeling it. The helicopter heading our way was a massive relief for the whole team. But in the next few moments, we also discovered that our command post had our location incorrectly plotted on the maps.

Our hopes turned to anger when we saw the helicopter begin to drop altitude about a mile north of our location. It slowly began to circle over a hilltop. I was trying to figure out what they were doing because I didn't think we had any personnel between our second team and us.

So, I radioed our second team, asking them what the helicopter was doing. (We also could not communicate with the helicopter.) The team leader from the second team told me that they were looking for us.

Then, I knew something was off. My team was essentially missing in action, and our support didn't know our coordinates. (I would find out later that our coordinates were not recorded by anyone at the command post when we were dropped. This was mainly due to how quickly the whole situation was evolving and how busy the command post was at the time.)

As I communicated with our second team, we decided that we would try to guide the helicopter into our location. So, I asked the team leader to look south from his location and watch for a quick flash of our light. We gave a few brief flashes and checked back in with him. He told me that they had not seen our light. He tried to give us a quick flash from his location and asked if we had seen their light. We had not.

We would later discover that we were in a location where we were out of the second team's line of sight due to the terrain. Given the situation, I tried to direct the helicopter into our location by guiding it hill-by-hill. The only problem was that I had to do this through our second team because, again, I did not have direct communication with the helicopter.

We watched as the helicopter flew to a new hilltop and began to hover and circle. I knew the bad guys would think that the helicopter was searching for them, making me more comfortable using our flashlights as signaling devices.

Eventually, all of our work paid off. The helicopter located us and descended. But they could not touch down where we were because of the terrain, so they had to hover about thirty feet above us as they offloaded the bottled water. We watched as it came down and landed with a big pop and splash.

The helicopter crew noted our coordinates and departed. When we got to the water drop, we found that many of the water bottles had exploded on impact, and we were only able to salvage a few full bottles. So, we each got several ounces of that refreshing clear liquid to savor, but the thirst from dehydration was definitely not quenched.

A few hours after dark, the decision was made to switch our teams out and bring us back to the command post. The command post first sent in a new team to watch over the crime scene until the following day when the crime-scene crews got there to process the area. Then the helicopter would fly back to our hilltop to gather us up and return us to the command post.

The pilot had to circle our hill for a few minutes to find a location where he was comfortable setting the helicopter down. Once he found his spot about two to three hundred yards away, we quickly made our way over to them. We loaded up, and the crew provided us with what had to be the best-tasting water I've ever drunk. It was just some off-brand bottled water, but I was so thirsty that it seriously tasted like water from a Rocky Mountain spring high in the Colorado Mountains.

Within minutes, we were back on the ground at the command post, and I met with my SWAT team commander to brief him on our piece of this huge puzzle and learn where we were overall. Our shooting victim was doing very well. His wound was from a pass-through shot in the fatty area on his side, right above his waistline. The bullet had caused a large laceration about an inch or so deep on his side.

At the scene of the shooting, there were shell casings and some clothing, but they didn't locate weapons or suspects. That large perimeter (remember, it was approximately one hundred square miles) had netted some results, but nobody they could prove to be our shooters.

They had captured over forty people throughout the desert who were either scouts, smugglers, or just regular illegal aliens who happened to be in the area on their way through. The Border Patrol processed these people and checked for gunshot residue, with no positive results.

Our federal partners, who were listening to different phones at the time and working on large-scale cases, were all working any and all of their sources in an attempt to figure out who the shooters were. Again, it was one of the largest responses I have ever seen from all different agencies. Everyone worked together toward a common goal.

To this day, the shooters have not been identified or captured. This may seem amazing to some, but it also speaks volumes about how vast this area is and how good these criminals are at using the terrain and their criminal network to their advantage.

It also speaks to the multitude of crimes and victims we never know about because stuff like this happens regularly but goes unreported. Every year, "John Doe" and "Jane Doe" remains are found in the open desert by hunters or people enjoying the outdoors. These people are often never identified, and their remains sit idle in a morgue.

Here is an interesting footnote and story connected with the area where the sheriff's shooting took place: within months of this shooting, there was another shootout in this same location. In this case, we received a 911 call from an individual who was later determined to be a member of a rip crew.

When he called 911, he told the operator that his friend had been shot and gave his location as "the same place where the sheriff was shot," meaning he was in the same mountain pass where our guy had been shot earlier in the year. As our operator was talking to him, they were able to get his GPS coordinates from his phone signal just before the phone call dropped.

When our first deputies arrived, both males were dead from large-caliber gunshot wounds. One male had a large gunshot wound in the center of his chest and was stuck to a saguaro cactus, almost standing erect. The other male was on the ground, also with a big gunshot wound to the chest. To the trained eye, it looked very much like a sniper shot from a long-range precision rifle.

There were never any suspects identified in this case, and it remains an unsolved murder. However, the rumor on the street was that the cartel wasn't happy with the rip crews interfering with the cartel's drug loads in this area. The cartel allegedly sent hitmen (or "sicarios") to help protect their loads. This story makes the most sense, mainly due to how the murders occurred.

13.

HEAD-ON RIP CREW

IT WAS LATE 2010, and we were in the thick of what had become a yearlong turf war with the Sinaloa cartel, headed by Joaquin Loera-Guzman, a.k.a. El Chapo. Our fight was not a war in the traditional sense of warfare, but as you know, it was a battle between law enforcement and a transnational criminal organization for turf, terrain, and smuggling routes that ran through these areas.

Being a criminal organization, the cartel did not recognize any lines or boundaries, including international and jurisdictional boundaries. The cartel considered any land within the areas where they smuggled drugs to be their land. They did not care if that land was in Mexico, the

United States, on Indian reservations, or was federal- or state-owned. It had been this way since the Pancho Villa days, when Pancho and his men, using guerilla tactics, rode into the United States using routes like these to carry out attacks.

In the opinion of the cartels, they owned these routes. Therefore, they controlled the land that these routes were on. Some of them will even tell you that this area is actually part of Mexico, and we gringos just moved the line. They think the U.S. moved the international border further south.

They are referring to the land acquisition by the U.S. from Mexico in the Treaty of Guadalupe Hidalgo in 1848, in which Mexico ceded approximately 525,000 square miles of land to the United States. The land acquired by the United States in this deal included all the areas these smuggling routes currently run through. The Mexicans have a very proud culture, descending from Aztec and Mayan warrior cultures, and they do not forget the past.

The cartels share this same pride, and they also happen to have billions of dollars on the line with the products they smuggle on these routes, so they are driven to maintain control of them. The cartels have moved metric tons of drugs, mostly going right into and through our county.

The Sinaloa cartel held control of Arizona borders. They used these rural routes because they knew there was a significantly lower risk of law enforcement detecting and intercepting their drug, weapon, and money loads. But although they had better chances of avoiding the cops on these routes, they still had a problem with greed—in both cartel members and those outside the cartel who saw an opportunity to rob them.

We often found that people working for the cartels would, in fact, be playing both sides. The scouts, packers, and guides would have inside knowledge of the smuggling routes and patterns. Hell, if they were connected enough, they would know precisely where the load was and where it was going. These bad guys would then coordinate with other bad guys to plan a robbery of the very drugs they were transporting.

The rip crews would wait for the drugs to enter our county. As the drugs got nearer to the small towns or major interstates, the rip crews would intercept them in what was usually a very fast, confrontational, and violent fashion.

Imagine your standard-issue bank robbery takedown, with several people bursting in with masks and guns, maybe firing off a few shots, and then taking everyone down as they rob the place. These rip-crew takedowns were much like that but mixed with a touch of an out-door-channel, big-game hunting show. They would often go into the desert, sneak by the scouts without detection, wait for the smugglers to arrive, and then jump them and take them down.

Quite frankly, these rip crews employed some of the same tactics we used to take down smugglers, except the rip crews were there to rob these drugs for their own use and resale. When the rip crews were fully operational in our area, not only would they use our tactics, they would sometimes even use cars, gear, and clothing to give the appearance that they were law enforcement.

Of course, the cartel did not particularly care to be robbed along their smuggling routes, so they employed armed security to accompany their loads. They also hired sicarios (or hitmen) on the smuggling routes in our area to seek out and counter anyone they believed to be on a rip crew. This made things even more dangerous for us. We were out there doing a legitimate law enforcement operation, but if we were mistaken as a rip crew by the cartel, we ran the risk of an all-out desert gun battle with the cartel security crews.

But we still had a job to do, and it was time for another

night operation in the Arizona desert. On this particular night, I was acting as the SWAT sergeant, and my team was focused on an area heavily used by a different branch of the Sinaloa cartel. This branch was run by a guy known for being much more confrontational and violent with law enforcement. We often used SWAT guys for operations like this because of the potential for violence.

This Sinaloa crew was almost exclusively known for having vehicle drug loads ("desert loaders"). These were the stolen vehicles that the cartels stole from the U.S., ran south into Mexico, loaded with drugs, and drove back north in the middle of the night to stash houses in our county. Tonight's mission would be a vehicle interdiction operation. We had information on a load headed our way and the most-likely routes they would be utilizing.

My crew for the night met up at a station located on the outskirts of the smuggling area we would work in. It was just after dusk, and we were all prepping our gear and doing what we did best—a whole lot of smack talking about who was the better cop and who would catch the bad guys. Sometimes, we even doled out more personal jokes about how much we liked each other's wives or whose moms we had relationships with.

I checked for any last-minute intelligence available

through either our other law enforcement partners or our confidential sources. This would allow me to adjust the operational parameters before we all mounted up and deployed for the night.

The information was not solid, but there was chatter that stolen trucks were running drugs north from the border on this night. Of course, this was the chatter almost every night, and, as usual, we did not have exact routes or times. We were somewhat taking a shot in the dark on exactly where we would set up, but we all knew the area and the smuggling groups well enough to make a reasonably good plan.

We made the team assignments for the night, which broke down to two-vehicle teams. Once we decided who would be in which vehicles and packed the gear, we were on our way.

As I mentioned, the cartel group operating in this corridor tended to be more confrontational and violent than other groups. Don't get me wrong—all of these cartel bastards were violent criminals, but there were also levels within these groups, and this group was known for being extremely aggressive.

On one occasion, a Border Patrol agent chased a stolen truck through the remote desert area in this corridor. At one point, he lost the vehicle and assumed they had gotten away. This agent continued working the area and tracking the routes he suspected they were traveling when he stumbled upon the truck. It had apparently broken down but was still occupied by bad guys.

As the agent got within about a hundred yards of the truck, he could see that there was a second truck that had met up with it. The agent saw that they were transferring items from one to the other. The agent was solo, and there was no backup for miles. He was outnumbered.

The agent also noticed that one of the bad guys was sporting what looked like an SKS rifle. As the bad guys continued to load items into the second truck, the guy with the rifle broke ranks from the others and started slowly walking toward the agent's vehicle, staring hard at the agent like a hawk who had spotted its prey.

As the bad guy got about ten yards in front of the stolen truck and still about eighty to ninety yards from the agent, he motioned to the agent with his hand. He waved his hand toward himself to tell the agent to come on, and he raised his SKS rifle a little higher and across his chest.

The agent had no doubt about what was going on. The bad guy was clearly challenging the agent, saying, "You want me? Come and get me." This agent made the smart choice and held his position. Within a few minutes, the bad guys all loaded up into the second truck and headed south toward Mexico.

This is just one example of how bold the cartel members in this corridor were, and quite frankly, we were not about to let actions like that go unchecked. We made this corridor our project. We would show these cartel bastards that they did not own this land, and we were not afraid to take them on.

I must admit that the story of what happened between the agent and the cartel member pissed me off. It felt like a direct threat and challenge to all law enforcement. The cartel members were telling us that they owned this corridor and we were not welcome there.

So what do you do when the wolves show up in your backyard and begin growling, circling, and snapping their teeth? Well, I decided we would walk right into the middle of the pack and show them that we were not afraid and would not give up easily.

It was now dark, and we were traveling south directly into the smuggling corridor. We traveled in tandem, with the lead vehicle using lights and the second vehicle with no lights. My team was the lead vehicle, so the second team was blacked out. It would have to travel just far enough back not to be lit up by the lights of the first vehicle.

We wanted the scouts to focus on and track the lead vehicle with its lights on. Then, as we reached the specific area where we wanted to work, the second vehicle would pull off and start sneaking in while the lead vehicle continued on as a distraction.

Being in the lead vehicle, we traveled several miles further south, eventually pulling into a ranch and turning off our lights as if this was our final destination. We gave it a few minutes to ensure the scouts watching would discount us as locals. We then left, lights out, and traveled back the way we had just come until we reached our insertion point into the open desert area of the corridor. We began our slow and methodical travel on four-wheel-drive roads directly into the heart of the smuggling route.

As we made our way in, our first vehicle team was about fifteen to twenty minutes ahead of us, traveling into the area where we would make our final stopping and intercept points.

I was in the front passenger seat, looking intently through my night-vision goggles as we traveled through the open Arizona desert. When traveling this way, everyone has to stay on their toes and pay extra attention to their surroundings—especially given the potential for violence in this corridor.

We had to ensure that scouts did not spot us or that smugglers who knew we were coming would not run into us. Or that smugglers would mistake us for a rip crew, which automatically kicked up the potential for violence a few notches. So, I intensely scanned everything around us, but it was fairly dark out, with only a little ambient light from the moon and stars.

As we crept along, we had our windows down to hear the surrounding desert. It is amazing how tuned in you become to your other senses while operating on night vision. You hear every little noise—coyotes howling like a group of banshees in the distance, a mouse scurrying through brush as it breaks branches and steps through leaves, or the low rumble of a vehicle engine as it travels through the desert terrain.

One of my team members broke the radio silence to check our location and status. I gave our approximate location and advised him that we were still making our way into the area. The team member wanted to verify their location, which was at a checkpoint that we had set up. Then, he asked if we were near them. I told him we were still approximately five minutes out from their location and would be there in minutes.

I then got another very inquisitive radio transmission

asking me to verify that I was not at or near their current position. We were often able to determine our exact location by landmarks. So, based on landmarks near us, I gave my lead vehicle our current position.

In response, my lead vehicle team asked if any "friendlies" were in the area. In other words, was there any possibility that other law enforcement was present in the corridor?

At this time, cartel-chasing had become the popular thing to do with many different law enforcement agencies—agencies that had normally never been part of this fight. We had the alphabet soup of federal agencies, state agencies, and local agencies all running around the deserts in our county, attempting to run their own interdiction operations.

When we worked as task forces, where we would all be involved in the communication and decision-making on such operations, it worked great, and we appreciated the help. Nonetheless, we had ongoing blue-on-blue problems. "Blue-on-blue" refers to those instances when cops would intercept cops, each thinking that the others were the bad guys. However, some agencies would often operate autonomously within our county, making our job even more difficult.

Most times, they did not do this maliciously, but rather because they had leadership within those agencies who did not want to share intelligence or information, fearing that others would compromise information or informants. Other times, we had to deal with egos. This fight had taken the national stage as a huge political platform. It received a lot of media coverage, so some of these agencies or leaders were chasing a little bit of the limelight.

Either way, we would often spend hours working our way into areas to intercept the cartels, only to have some other agency that had decided to work in that area come through and completely blow our operation.

Not that we were territorial. Believe me, there was plenty of work to go around, but we had systems in place to ensure that we would avoid any blue-on-blue situations. There were many heated discussions behind closed doors after these incidents.

I told my lead team that there should not be any other law enforcement in the area because I had talked to members of our federal partners and Border Patrol, who also worked there. But as I said, a blue-on-blue situation couldn't be ruled out.

Within seconds, my lead vehicle team came over the radio with a slight panic in their voice. When an adrenaline dump shoots through your veins in a situation like this, it causes an instantaneous increase in your heart rate, dilation of your eyes, and sometimes a few octaves increase in your voice. My team in the other vehicle shouted that bad guys were there in a truck. The bad guys had spotted our team, and my team was now chasing the blacked-out bad-guy truck through the desert.

What I did not know, and only found out after the chase was over, is that the vehicle team had reached our first rendezvous point and parked to wait for us. Within minutes, they heard a truck traveling near their location. As the vehicle got closer, they held their position, believing it could be my team approaching their position.

Within minutes, they saw a quad-cab truck stop within fifty yards of their location. As they were asking us questions over the radio, one of our team members watched all four doors of what ended up being a stolen truck open almost simultaneously, and four people exited the truck. Again, the vehicle was operating without lights, and our guys were all operating with night-vision goggles.

The first thing that was very apparent, even under night vision, was that the four men appeared to be wearing some type of tactical gear, like plate carriers.

As I discussed in Chapter 8, a plate carrier is a vest-type

carrier system with heavy ballistic plates inserted into it that are rated to take handgun and rifle hits. It generally has Molle loops sewn onto the entire vest, allowing you to mount pouches and accessories on it, such as extra magazine carriers, handcuffs, radio pouches, and pouches designed to carry medical supplies. If you envision any modern-day soldiers, especially any special operations teams, you will often see them wearing a plate carrier like this.

Plate carriers were the preferred equipment for our team, as they allowed for good mobility and ballistic protection from both handguns and rifles. Mobility is a crucial component when operating in vehicles. Too much equipment or bulky gear can cause problems getting in and out of the vehicle and to your equipment quickly.

So my lead vehicle team watched the four men exit the truck wearing these plate carriers, and they saw the men start to relieve themselves under the clear moonlit night.

At that point, another important detail became immediately noticeable to our people. These guys all seemed to be carrying long guns or rifles slung and hanging in front of them, much like we carry our rifles. However, there was one big difference. These long guns had a very distinct outline and shape. They were carrying the weapon of choice for cartels and bad guys in our area—the AK-47, otherwise known as the "cuerno de chivo" or "horn of the goat."

One final detail that added to the overall picture was that our guys could hear the music playing in the truck. They were playing those Mexican narcocorridos that are ever-popular among the cartels.

Our guys were rapidly processing everything in front of them to decide what to do next. Their hasty planning process was cut short when one of the bad guys saw our lead vehicle in the moonlight and our guys standing outside of it, looking at them.

A bad guy yelled in Spanish for his team to get back in their truck. Our team also scrambled into their vehicle and turned their lights on, only to see the stolen truck loaded with what appeared to be a sicario (rip crew) inside, spinning its tires and speeding off across the open desert terrain away from our guys. From this point, it became an old-fashioned vehicle pursuit, except we knew why our bad guys were running, and we also knew that they were heavily armed and prepared.

As my team listened to the radio traffic to find out what was going on, we continued to drive blacked-out and made our way toward the area where our guys were actively chasing the bad guys. But it only took a few minutes for the darkness of the desert night to combine with the dust kicked up by the bad guys, and our lead vehicle had lost a visual on the bad-guy truck.

Meanwhile, my team was getting close to their location, driving somewhat slowly and methodically. My partner concentrated intently on the four-wheel-drive road we were traveling on because we were still blacked out and using night vision. As he drove, I also focused intensely on the road ahead, acting as another set of eyes for him.

Then, I saw just the ever-so-slightly shiny glint of something ahead of us on the same road. It was hard to make out what I was seeing, and the green of the night-vision goggles, combined with the shadows cast by the ambient light of the moonlight, did not make it any easier.

I asked my partner if he saw what I saw. He said he saw something but could not determine exactly what it was. We slowed a bit more, doing everything we could to make out what we saw through our night vision.

Within seconds, we both exclaimed, "Shit! It's a truck!" And it was coming straight at us, head-on.

My partner cranked the wheel hard to the left, and

luckily, the bad guy driving the stolen truck did the same, almost as if it were a well-choreographed dance with the two trucks. We narrowly missed hitting the other truck in a head-on collision, and as they passed us, the stolen truck punched it and began to travel cross country to get away.

We spun around and started to give chase when we saw the truck's brake lights activate and violently bounce up and down, just before the lights came to a hard stop. A dust cloud formed around the truck, accompanied by a loud crashing and metal-ripping sound. I knew that what I had just seen was the bad-guy truck getting into a wreck. We could hear the engine still revving loudly, but it was not moving.

Both our lead vehicle team and my team drove up on the stolen truck at almost the same time, only to find that it had wrecked into a small wash and was stuck. We slowly approached the vehicle, not knowing if we still had bad guys inside or not. All four doors were open, the nar-cocorridos were still playing, an AK-47 was sitting on the ground outside the front passenger door, and the truck was unoccupied.

This meant that we had four bad guys out there, and at least three of them were armed with AK-47s.

We immediately set up a small security perimeter

around our vehicles and the stolen truck, preparing to defend ourselves if the bad guys launched an assault on us to get their vehicle back. We weren't sure if they were nearby, had any other bad guys in the area assisting them, or if they were determined enough to try to confront us. Our team communicated with our dispatch center to let them know what was going on, and a couple of backup units headed our way to assist us if the bad guys came back for a fight.

As we cleared the stolen truck and began to search it, one team member took the AK-47, cleared it of any ammunition, and rendered it safe. He placed it into one of our vehicles to be taken to the station and processed as evidence.

The procedure was to take the guns we had seized and run them through the Bureau of Alcohol, Tobacco, Firearms and Explosives (BATFE) eTrace database. This database allowed us to trace the origins of each seized weapon. Since the BATFE debacle known as "Operation Fast and Furious," we were especially interested in the source of firearms involved in smuggling or cartel activities.

After running it through the database, we could not associate this seized AK-47 with any other crime, so it simply remained in our custody as another piece of evidence from our ongoing battle against these cartels.

Within an hour, we had our backup on the scene. A tow truck also arrived to load the stolen truck and take it to one of the many local tow yards. Most of the time, these stolen vehicles would be so abused and damaged after the cartels used them for smuggling that the insurance companies would write them off as a total loss, and thus they never returned to their owners.

After intercepting and confiscating dozens of these vehicles over the years, I can honestly say that the best bet for anyone who has their vehicle stolen and used by the cartel is just to get the insurance payout. The cartel members run these stolen trucks like they are running a Baja race. We learned very quickly which brand of truck could outperform the others. I have seriously been amazed at some of the abuse I witnessed these vehicles go through as cartel tools.

With the truck on its way to a tow yard, the AK-47 in our possession, and the bad guys doing what they do best in these encounters, which is to get away, it was time to call it a day. It may seem discouraging to have the bad guys get away like this, but we focused on the positive in this game. I mean, we had to, or we would lose our minds. We had to look at the fact that we got their truck and one of their weapons off the streets. And, inevitably, they always left a little evidence behind that gave us more intelligence on our enemy.

Smuggler vehicles had traveled some of these areas so heavily that the dirt had become pulverized and powdered into a fine silt that would nearly create a smoke screen when you drove through it. We referred to it as "moon dust," and it was almost like driving or walking through a foot of brown baby powder. It would turn you, your vehicle, and any of your equipment into what looked like a brown, powder-coated donut.

The only good thing about this moon dust was that it showed foot tracks very well. So, of course, we did a sweep and short-tracking operation to see if we could locate any sign of our bad guys hiding in the area before we left. We tried to locate shoe tracks on the dry desert floor.

We immediately located the "foot sign" of the bad guys who fled the stolen truck. A couple of them ran away together, and the other two ran in different directions. We tracked the footprints and determined that these guys had not circled back or stopped at all. The best working theory was that they were probably still running.

With no fresh sign of the bad guys, no indication they

were still in the area, and no reason to stay at this spot, we called it a night.

Both teams headed back to our station to debrief and head home. These debriefing sessions were really the only way to improve and ensure our people's highest performance and safety. These debriefs were open and honest, with everyone leaving their egos at the door to ensure we had good conversations and feedback to improve ourselves.

In the debrief, we went over the events that took place and how we reacted or performed. We evaluated and critiqued how the operation went to correctly identify any mistakes we had made, things we could have done better, and any gaps we would need to focus on in future operations.

It was a constant work in progress for all of us. If you think about it, there was no roadmap, and we were laying new foundations for a type of cop work that was not even a thing for local cops until this point.

Once we debriefed, we went home to get some rest and family time and prepare to do it all over again.

14.

NO LONGER ALONE

OUR COUNTY WAS NOW IN the national limelight for our ongoing battle with the Mexican cartels—mainly because we were not right on the U.S. and Mexico border. Instead, we were sixty-five miles north of the border. Mix in the occasional desert shootout, homicide, or pursuit, and we had become one of the focal points for the whole smuggling and illegal immigration problems.

We had everything from national and local news channels to foreign print media coming to our county to see what was going on. Our sheriff was very vocal about both the problems we faced from the Mexican cartels and the complete lack of support that we received from the White House and Washington D.C. He often used these news outlets to call out the country's politicians. All of this added up to a whole lot of attention and coverage.

By this time, I had been promoted again and was serving as the lieutenant over the anti-smuggling efforts. I was well-briefed and knowledgeable on the cartels and the history of our fight because I had done the job since early 2000. Growing up in and around Mexican culture and cartel influence gave me a decent working knowledge of that side as well. So, I became one of the spokesmen for our agency on matters related to the cartels and the smuggling problems.

It had become the norm for me to take a news crew or a reporter out on our missions as we battled the smugglers. Typically, we would take them to locations just off of the interstate. I would often take them to Interstate 8, which starts in our county and runs all the way to San Diego, and show them "load-out spots." These were places where the smugglers (usually backpackers) would stop to wait for a transport vehicle to pick them up with their drugs.

When this took place, the smugglers would leave their trash behind. We would find the remnants of black water bottles, Pedialyte bottles, food wrappers, and toiletries.

This trash would include large burlap sacks, which, up until that point, had contained two or three bundles of marijuana inside to form a large, square burlap backpack. The backpacks would have two large strips cut from Mexican blankets, and they would attach them as shoulder straps.

Other common trash items were the carpet booties designed to fit over a smuggler's entire shoe. The booties were used to hide their footprints as they backpacked the drugs north from Mexico. They were important to the backpackers because Border Patrol agents were excellent trackers. Smugglers knew that to outsmart the agents, they would need to do a damn good job hiding their footprints in whatever way possible. But Border Patrol agents were so good that they eventually learned to distinguish carpet bootie tracks.

Our county was like a smuggling hub and, at times, must have looked like Grand Central Station with all the activity. Some areas were so heavily used by the drug traffickers that there would be layers of trash for an eighth- to a quarter-mile in any direction. We had trash on top of trash on top of trash.

The news reporters would marvel at this fact, snap their pictures, and continually ask how it was possible.

We would always explain to them the sheer volume of smuggling in and through our county. We gave them the low-down on precisely what was going on, how the cartels operated, and why our county was vital terrain for the cartel. Each and every time, these reporters would act surprised and wonder why they had never known this before.

One of the most common questions I would get from reporters was, "Why isn't this all over the news?" It seemed a little odd to me that they would be asking that question, but I felt they were mostly just thinking aloud, and the question was rhetorical.

Reporters would also ask the million-dollar question of why the federal government is not doing anything about it. My typical reply would be to explain that this is why we are showing them what is truly going on—so that they could report on it and, hopefully, Washington D.C. would step up and help.

These constant media feeds, combined with our sheriff blasting Washington D.C. for their lack of support, finally resulted in some help. The Border Patrol National Tactical Team showed up from Del Rio, Texas. Apparently, there had been enough pressure that the top levels of Border Patrol sent this team to our county to fight the smuggling and cartels specifically. While we had never worked with these guys, we had worked with some local BORTAC elements, and these were top-notch dudes. So, we welcomed the additional help.

During this same time frame, we participated in extensive, ongoing joint operations with our state and local partners and with several of our federal partners, including Border Patrol, Bureau of Land Management (BLM), Immigration and Customs Enforcement (ICE), and Homeland Security Investigations (HSI). These operations covered a large area and required coordinated efforts that involved weeks of planning and sometimes hundreds of cops from all of these agencies.

We had such a large volume of smuggling traffic that we formed a task force consisting of Border Patrol, Homeland Security Investigations, and our agency. The task force became known as the West Desert Task Force because that was the main smuggling corridor we focused on.

We combated the cartels so successfully that we became the national model for fighting the smuggling problem. But as successful as we were, we were still being overrun by the cartels in the West Desert.

CONFUSION AND CHAOS

On the large joint operations, the planning phase would include teams being assigned to specific duties.

One specific assignment was on a mountaintop sur-veillance team—a listening post/observation post. These LP/OP teams usually consisted of two to four people. We would covertly insert a team into an area within the heart of the smuggling route, and they would then hike their way to high points that overlooked the smuggling areas. These teams were basically doing exactly what the cartel scouts were doing.

The LP/OP teams often would be covertly sharing a hill with the cartel scouts, or they would have scouts on a hill nearby. When these teams moved into their locations and occupied their post, it was essential for them to limit their noise and light. If they did not, the scouts in the area would easily detect them. They were right in the scout battlespace—the location the cartel scouts were respon-sible for securing—and the team had to work without giving their position away.

Typically, they would have the difficult task of hiking up the hill with a good amount of gear and technology and then setting it up to monitor their assigned area. On several occasions, an LP/OP team had a scout so close to their location that they had to shut off communications (radios or phones) and lay completely still on the side of a hill in the rocks and brush until the scout left.

Another piece to this complex puzzle was the takedown teams. These teams were exactly what they sounded like—teams designated to take down or arrest the smugglers or packers. Takedown teams typically had six to eight people, mainly consisting of tactical team members with experience in takedown and tracking.

These teams were responsible for getting out on foot, moving into a specific and usually predetermined location (like a choke point), and intercepting the backpackers. They would do this under the watchful eyes of the LP/OP crew, who acted in an overwatch position and guided the takedown team to their target group.

However, telling the two groups apart would sometimes get confusing because the takedown team was so close to the smuggler crew. So, we used technology to our advantage and carried specific tactical lights. The lights served as a marker so our LP/OPs could distinguish the good guys from the bad guys.

We would often also have either a helicopter or a high-flying ISR (intelligence, surveillance, and reconnaissance) plane in the air to assist us. The air support would locate the backpackers and then provide laser markers for the takedown team to quickly identify and move in on them.

The LP/OP and air teams often worked in unison to guide the takedown team, getting in nice and close to the packer crew. Most of the time, they could even tell us if we were moving in on an armed long-gun crew or if it appeared that the group was not carrying long guns.

Once the takedown team was close to the backpackers, there would be a few last-minute preparations and communications. Then the takedown team would move hard and fast. They would toss noise-flash diversionary devices known as "flash bangs" to disorient and confuse the packer group. Then they would shine bright lights on the faces to further confuse the packers and provide our team with a tactical advantage.

This strategy provided an element of surprise and chaos that the packers were not expecting. Each time, the result would be a quick takedown of the group with little to no resistance, and almost everyone would get caught.

Watching the utterly chaotic scenes play out in front of me, I often wondered what must be going through the smugglers' minds. I mean, think about it. It's the middle of the night. You and your compadres are walking through the dark Arizona desert in an area controlled by, for the most part, your fellow smugglers. Then, out of nowhere … BOOM!! Flashing lights, people yelling in English and Spanish, and the complete quiet erupts into total mayhem.

A takedown always made me chuckle inside a little because I could see the disorientation, confusion, and those "what in the hell?" looks on the packers' faces as we attacked. I also loved the fact that we beat them at their own game.

The vehicle teams, which were still in play on these ground operations, were the third critical component of the overall operation. Vehicles were important. We used them to deliver the observation and takedown teams, act as rescues for ground teams, and transport smugglers and drugs once a takedown took place.

The vehicle teams would also have a marked patrol car that we could use to make traffic stops. Most of the time, we used these stops as a form of terrain denial. For instance, there were times when we wanted the scouts to identify the presence of law enforcement to ensure that the smugglers would steer clear of that area. So, we would have the marked units conduct consistent traffic stops in that location. We referred to this as making an area "hot" or "heating it up."

The smugglers had much land to use, and we typically did not have an exact route that they would take. Making an area "hot" helped narrow down the places we would have to focus on. Additionally, the roads, trails, and four-wheel-drive roads that the smugglers took splintered into several other route options as they got closer to Interstate 8. It became very important to "funnel" them into a region where we wanted them to go.

BLUE-ON-BLUE IN THE ALPHABET SOUP

As I said, all of this movement, manpower, and resources took planning and preparation to do it safely and effectively. It also took everyone sticking to their assignments and doing their particular job to have overall success.

We did a pretty good job with all of this as a whole, but things got off track every once in a while. There would be an agency that felt like they didn't have a significant enough task or wanted to do a particular function, and this would lead to some missed steps during an operation. It was challenging to mix that many agencies—including the alphabet soup of federal agencies—and have everyone stick to one script and plan.

But we were all on the same team and fighting the same bad guys, so if everyone stuck to the script, it worked pretty well, and we all enjoyed the success of a good operation.

Eventually, we did enough of these operations for people to find their groove. We knew which people and teams were good at which jobs, and we assigned them accordingly. For example, some groups had been doing takedowns for a while and were pretty effective. You could take that same crew and stick them on an LP/OP team, and they might not be as effective in that position. It was a matter of putting people where they fit best.

Working these operations had become the cool thing to do because of both the local and national coverage. Agencies started coming out of the woodwork to "help with the issues" and jump in on these operations. Sometimes this was good, and sometimes it only led to more problems.

Some agencies had not done this type of work or had the proper equipment or training. Additionally, some agencies wanted to do specific jobs or tasks, but they would not be assigned to those tasks because other units were already in place. We were not better than anyone else, and no team was better than another, but it was all about mission and objective and where we all fit best. But when agencies didn't get what they wanted, it did not sit well with them and caused issues during the actual operations.

I remember several occasions when we would have an LP/OP spot a group of backpackers and provide their location coordinates. Our air assets would get in the air and, using the coordinates, would locate the group from the air. The designated ground and takedown teams would start to move into position to jump the packer group, arrest them, and confiscate their drugs.

Then, just as the plan was coming together, the LP/OP would notify us that another armed group was in the same area. We would have to contact our TOC (Tactical Operations Center). The TOC would have to do a roll call over the radio to figure out if these were good guys there by mistake or bad guys there to do harm.

You have to keep in mind that we were still dealing with the problem of rip crews working in this area. On more than one occasion, we actually jumped rip crews who were on their way to rob a packer crew. So these rogue agencies would look just like a rip crew, and we would end up in a blue-on-blue situation.

Deconfliction is a system used by law enforcement to ensure that the case they are working on does not conflict with the same one another law enforcement agency is working on. Using deconfliction significantly reduces the chance of a blue-on-blue situation.

BORDER PATROL BADASSERY

Over time, smuggler takedowns became routine for us. We did them consistently, using all the resources we've discussed. When the national BORTAC team arrived, they were already familiar with these tactics. They had also been employing the same tactics and techniques.

Let me tell you, I have worked with a lot of tactical teams throughout my years, and the Border Patrol BORTAC team had some of the toughest and best dudes I have ever had the pleasure of working with. They were well-trained, disciplined, and on point with their tactics and techniques.

That said, the one piece the Del Rio BORTAC team hadn't had as much exposure to until that point was the vehicle component. How we used our vehicles covertly to sneak into areas for personnel drops and takedowns was fascinating to them. And how well they could operate on foot and track human beings were just as fascinating to us.

So as we sat in a planning meeting one day, drafting one

of the large operations I described, the Del Rio BORTAC Commander and I had the opportunity to meet and talk shop. We talked about some of the issues we were having during these operations and how some agencies could not get out of their own way.

The commander, who I will just call J, suggested we team up. We met after the planning meeting to discuss what it would look like and how we could use this as an opportunity to learn from each other and do some great work together.

The plan was to pair our team leaders together, having two-man teams with one BORTAC leader and one of my leaders. During these operations, they would co-lead a small unit or squad with a specific assignment (like a takedown team).

We would also team up one of our guys with one of their guys as an LP/OP team because they were very skilled at sneaking in, setting up a hiding location, and then acting as spotters for the takedown teams.

Lastly, we would pair up in the vehicles and act as rescue, takedown, insertion, or chase teams. This is where we would get the opportunity to teach the BORTAC guys a little about how we operated in vehicles. It was an absolute win/win because we learned a lot, taught them a little, and put a good dent in cartel operations.

Another advantage to our teaming up was that both teams had access to and used some of their own technology. We began sharing this information as we worked together more and more. BORTAC operated much like a top-tier military unit and had access to a lot of technology and equipment. This access really helped us in our mission to disrupt and dismantle these cartels.

We would combine our intelligence and assets, sharing and discussing openly. If we were not working on a joint operation where we were teamed up, we would be communicating all the time. Essentially, we discussed where and when we would be working to ensure that we were not screwing each other up by stumbling into each other's work.

This was not a general discussion either, as we had built a deep trust between the teams and even friendships between team members. We had them on our electronics system to receive alerts on some of our devices to monitor and record activity. We also provided them with sensitive intelligence that we received from confidential informants. We even gave them specific information on inbound loads or stash houses that we could not go after in hopes that they would take them off.

This level of cooperation was not the norm—especially as it relates to Border Patrol. The men and women on the ground were the best people I have ever worked with. But, the politics within some of the management—especially the D.C. level politics of Border Patrol—were some of the worst I have ever had to deal with. It made working with some parts of the Border Patrol very difficult. There were even instances where we would have to work twice as hard just to avoid having a major case screwed up because of egos. This was the exception, though, and not the norm.

Back to our Del Rio team. We had successfully built a working model for fighting the cartel in our county, and we had done exceptionally well at terrain denial. We were able to cause some disruption to the cartels in our area. We forced them to establish new routes, use different routes, and, in some cases, even avoid our area altogether.

We were hitting the smugglers, the scouts, and the re-suppliers. Meanwhile, the investigative arm of our large task force was putting together larger cases against the cartel bosses based on our enforcement actions. However, we did not totally eradicate them from our area. Like any money-making criminal organization, they just kept on pushing their product.

15.

THE SLEEPY MONSTER

ON A WARM ARIZONA NIGHT, with just a sliver of moon out, we were teamed up with our BORTAC brothers for one of these interdiction operations. I was paired up with a BORTAC team leader, who I will call Pablo.

Pablo was a quiet professional, and I learned a lot about who BORTAC was and what they were about by spending time with him during these long overnight operations. I mean, you always kind of know what other tactical teams do, but BORTAC is a whole different level of a tactical team. They operate very similar to a top-tier military special operations forces group in how they are structured, select personnel, and work.

The biggest difference with BORTAC is with the open-terrain work they do, which is why we teamed up with them. We were doing the same stuff, just on a smaller scale. These guys had mastered the ground game of maneuvering on and capturing bad guys. Pablo's teammates were quiet professionals who were solid in their tactics and techniques.

Pablo and I teamed up as a vehicle team, which gave us the mobility to respond to whatever area our crew would be working. We were all designated as vehicle teams for this particular operation. The plan was to first drop in the LP/OP teams so they could move to their spots for the night. Our team would then stage in several different areas in our particular area of operation.

We also had air support on many of the operations, which, typically speaking, would be a helicopter with a crew. We relied heavily on the technology of both our LP/OP crew and our air units. The technology they had available to spot people, vehicles, and just about anything else was great, and this would give us our tactical advantage.

However, the only problem with the helicopter in this area was the noise signature. As I've said before, sound carries far on a dark and quiet night in the valleys of the Arizona desert.

Imagine sitting by yourself on a lonely mountaintop with nothing around for miles. It is dark all around you. The desert is alive with small creatures and bugs moving, the occasional coyote howling, and sometimes random gunfire in the distance. But other than that, it is hushed. This becomes your normal setting, and you become very aware of sounds that do not fall into that normal category.

Now, in the distance, you can hear the ever-so-slight thud of helicopter blades as they spin to create the lift to keep that bird in the air. Depending on the type of helicopter, you can hear and even slightly feel a little bop, bop, bop, bop, bop, bop in your ears and chest.

If you have never experienced it, you do not immediately recognize what it is. Sometimes, because sound bounces around in the surrounding mountain ranges, it will remain just this slight thud in the distance until the helicopter is right on top of you. Either way, the experienced cartel scout knows exactly what the sound is, and it immediately sets off alarms for them.

You have to remember that their lives depended on doing their job correctly. To miss a helicopter flying through their area would be a big no-no because an aircraft can easily spot and interdict their precious drug and human loads. Depending on terrain, cartel scouts could call out our helicopter ten minutes before they even got to the area where they could effectively work for those of us on the ground.

Knowing this, we had to have specific strategies to keep our helicopter close by and ready to go. With the number of mountains in the area and the terrain's complexity, we relied a little on the cover of the mountains, knowing our scout locations, and on human nature.

By putting our helicopter in that area well ahead of our operation's start time, they could make their rounds through the mountains and valleys. The scouts would call them out while they took cover and hid. Then the helicopter would make its way to a predetermined and hidden location to stage for the operation.

The scouts would lose sight of the helicopter and could no longer hear it, so they would come back out. With the helicopter gone, like street-corner drug dealers in any neighborhood, they would slowly creep back out, call the coast clear, and get back to their normal business.

This particular operation covered such a large area that each team had a designated section they were responsible for. We were the takedown team for our zone, starting just east of our county line with Maricopa County and running east along Interstate 8 for about twenty miles.

We had designated locations along the interstate to sneak into with blacked-out vehicles and then move into a hiding spot to wait. We would wait for the LP/OPs to spot smugglers moving through the area, whether by vehicle or on foot. Then, we would coordinate with our LP/OPs and air assets and move in on the smugglers to take them down and arrest them. We did this successfully so often during this timeframe that it wasn't if it would happen, but rather when it would happen.

Our teams all got into position and settled in. We first went through a roll call of our team to ensure that everyone was in their position, ready to go, and had good radio communication. As the team leader, I then reported back to the TOC to inform them that we were in place and operational. We also notified the LP/OPs.

At this point, it became simply a waiting game, as we did not have specific information or intelligence on a load coming through. But we were working some of the frequently used routes by the smugglers. We identified these routes based on our fieldwork, traveling, and monitoring those routes ourselves. We also had technology in place to observe some of these routes remotely.

We used other technology for terrain denial, which I talked about earlier. The technology would alert us to the presence of activity, and we could then deploy assets such as marked patrol cars or aircraft to a particular area. This would solicit a response from the cartel scouts, who would notify vehicle or backpacker crews of our presence. Doing this in one location would cause the smugglers to shift to a secondary route. These secondary routes would be the routes we had under surveillance, with our teams ready to take the smugglers down when they were deep enough into our web.

As we waited, Pablo and I talked about life and work. We discussed our histories and our craft. I learned quite a bit about the history of BORTAC, how they operated, where they operated, and just how tough these guys were. I also learned a lot about Pablo, and it was always interesting how much we were alike, with him having a deep love for his job and his country. We had some great fellowship on these long nights, and I gained a lot of respect for Pablo and his entire crew.

We worked through this night, sometimes fighting what we referred to as "the sleepy monster." This fictitious monster would sneak up on you during these operations, get you in a figurative chokehold, and put you to sleep.

Your body would give in to the fatigue and quiet of the overnight shift, and you would start to drift to sleep.

You know that timeframe when your eyes become so heavy that you fight to keep them open, every once in a while you lose the battle, and as you start to nod off, your body jerks you awake with a flinch? If you succumb to the sleepy monster, you become fair game to laughs, snickers, and the occasional practical joke.

As Pablo and I sat there fighting the sleepy monster, a call came over the radio. Adrenaline raced through our veins and immediately turned us from tired to wide awake. One of the team members responsible for monitoring the technology indicated that we had some activity. It was unknown if an animal had triggered the alarm or if there was actually a human moving through. Our LP/OPs were now laser-focused on this particular area to find out.

The LP/OP had technology that would allow them to identify smugglers moving in the vicinity quickly, and they now had their eyes on a group of backpackers. Before long, they reported that the backpacker group was positive for carrying drugs. The LP/OP team could see that the backpackers were carrying the very distinctive, large, square "marijuana backpacks."

As the LP/OP team continued to monitor and report

on the backpacker group, we started to coordinate the movement of our vehicle teams. We slowly moved and maneuvered teams to shrink our coverage area down and focus on the vicinity that contained the smugglers.

Typically, the backpackers would work their way toward Interstate 8, which would be their goal line. They would then stop and wait along the interstate for the person or people responsible for picking them up and transporting them to a local stash house. So as this group of smugglers headed north through the desert and toward the interstate, our LP/OP team kept them under surveillance.

One by one, our vehicle teams moved closer to the area where we felt they would "load out," which is what we called the loading of their drug packs into the transport vehicles. Usually, we would know by the trail they were taking, or by the particular area they were moving through, approximately where they would end up on the interstate.

As the backpacker group approached the interstate, they stopped short, staging approximately twenty-five yards from the roadway on the south side of the interstate. When the LP/OP team reported that the backpackers had all stopped, taken their packs off, and sat down, the next part of the operation started: our helicopter crew fired up the helicopter.

Once airborne, they headed to the location where the backpackers were sitting with the drugs. The helicopter crew flew blacked out to maintain some form of stealth. We knew that the helicopter could not cover its sound, but if they flew blacked-out and under night vision, they had at least some level of stealth as they moved toward the target.

When the helicopter was a mile or so out, the LP/OP activated their lasers that were only visible under night vision to mark the backpackers' location for the helicopter and our vehicle teams sitting in slightly-higher, elevated positions or close to the packers. As the LP/OP team lit up the target packer crew with the laser, the helicopter locked in on them.

Meanwhile, our vehicle teams had all snuck into the area and met at a rally point about a mile away, very close to the interstate. Pablo and I discussed the takedown plan. We provided our teams with the order of vehicles to travel to the final stopping point, park, and get out on foot to move in on the packers. We also discussed the method and tactics for the takedown for this group. After some quick discussion, fast planning, and final assignments, we mounted up in our vehicles and headed to our final staging location.

While this was going on, our LP/OP team had the packers under surveillance and marked their location with the laser again. Our helicopter moved in and was now over the top of the packer group.

The first time we did this type of takedown, I fully expected the group to take off running as soon as they heard the helicopter nearby. The weird thing was that this did not happen. Instead, they all hunkered down a little closer to each other and hid underneath the large mesquite and Palo Verde trees that lined the side of Interstate 8. It was the same tonight. The group stayed right where they were.

The sound of the helicopter provided our vehicle teams with great sound cover as we drove down the interstate toward the packers. The chop, chop, chop of the blades overhead almost completely drowned out all other sounds, so we parked about fifty yards from where the laser lit up a small group of trees. Our vehicle teams dismounted, and we gathered for a final radio and gear check to ensure that everyone was ready to go.

Again, all of my guys were mixed in with the Del Rio BORTAC guys, and for these takedowns, we were operating by the BORTAC rules of engagement. Those rules called for us to sneak up to the group under cover of darkness and use night vision. Then, as we got within feet of the packers, BORTAC would deploy a noise-flash diversionary device. It would completely disorient the group and allow us the element of surprise in a violently fast takedown. (Remember that these groups typically had armed security people to protect them from the rip crews.)

Pablo and I led our team slowly away from the interstate, onto the dirt shoulder, and toward the trees. The LP/OP team had shut off their laser, and the helicopter crew activated their laser, which we could clearly see under our night vision. The green laser shot straight down in a beam from the helicopter and hit the trees, where it broke into scattered pieces that shimmered like a light hitting a disco ball on the dance floor.

As we approached the trees, this shimmering laser light allowed us to see the backpackers gathered around the base of a large mesquite tree. Some of the packers were sitting on their packs, some were sitting on the ground, and at least one was standing up.

We could tell from their demeanor that they were not very concerned with the helicopter overhead. Thinking back, I believe it was because the aircraft was completely blacked out. The packers must have thought that the helicopter didn't see them if it wasn't lighting them up with the large light attached to it (known as the "night sun").

We closed in further, and we could actually hear the smugglers talking amongst themselves. We were creeping up, like a lion slowly sneaking up to pounce on its prey drinking at the water pond, to within feet of the entire backpacker crew sitting under the tree.

Pablo stopped and turned to face the team. He held up his hand, which held a flashbang, and moved it from side to side to ensure that all members saw that he was preparing to deploy it. Then, in an exaggerated manner, he pulled the pin so that we could all see that it was time to go live.

These flashbangs operate much like a grenade—you have to pull the pin to allow the spoon to be "unlocked." You hold the spoon in your hand, and when you toss the flashbang, the spoon is free to spring off of the device, activating the (typically) one-and-one-half second fuse.

So once Pablo had pulled the pin, we knew that he would toss the flashbang into the group of backpackers. In just over a second, we would all experience the loud explosion, large flash, and huge smoke cloud from the device.

Pablo made a near-perfect underhand toss of the

flashbang into the middle of the packer group. As the flashbang was floating through the air, our team moved into place quickly. We had almost surrounded the tree when the quiet, dark night lit up with approximately seven million candela and around 170 decibels of "boom."

Let me give you an idea of how powerful this explosion actually is. An ordinary candle is one candela, so it is like seven million candles all lit up at once in about a forty-square-foot area. A jet engine is over 140 decibels, so the sound created is like firing up the loudest jet engine you can find in that same forty-square-foot area. When the flashbang detonates, you can imagine the surprise and confusion it creates.

We knew it was coming, but the packers weren't prepared to experience the full effects of the flashbang. A few of them stayed on the ground and went into a fetal or a completely facedown-surrender position, while others immediately began running. Our team now went "white light," which means we went from operating under night vision to using our weapon-mounted flashlights to light up the area and the packers.

Some team members quickly took the packers on the ground into custody as the other packers ran right into our team members who had surrounded the tree. There was a four-strand barbed-wire fence several feet south of the tree, and I watched as one of the packers ran right toward this fence.

Unfortunately for this guy, the bright light of the flashbang, followed by the bright flashlights, had rendered his vision useless, and he was running blindly into the night. Within seconds, I saw him hit the barbed-wire fence at full speed. The highest wire on the fence hit the packer just below his sternum, and he did one of the most amazing front flips I have ever seen and went right over the top of the fence.

This guy had done a flip-and-a-half, landing hard on his back on the other side of the fence. There was a loud thud as he hit the field dirt under the fence, and he let out a combination of exhalation and scream at the same time. As I moved toward him, I could see that he had either knocked himself out or had simply given up because he was not moving at all.

We took him into custody, but one packer had made a clean getaway and was being chased by both our ground guys and the helicopter. He was captured just down the interstate when he ran into one of our other teams headed to help us. They brought him back to our location, and all packers were accounted for.

We searched our captured packers for weapons, then walked them out to the edge of the interstate, where we lined them up, sitting down and handcuffed behind their backs. Under the tree, we found all of their marijuana backpacks. They were the typical twenty-five-pound bundles packed into burlap sacks to make fifty- to seventy-five-pound packs. Most of the burlap sacks still had sweat marks where they rubbed up against the back of the backpacker. We also located smuggler radios and solar panels.

We collected all of the evidence and brought it to the edge of the interstate. We had endured hours of waiting, only to be interrupted by minutes of pure adrenaline. Now, we had to settle down and start the long and tedious task of processing the evidence, transporting it, and securing it at the station.

We also had to interview and process the packers we had captured. This crew was charged with a multitude of felonies. We booked them into our county jail for possessing and transporting eight backpacks of marijuana, which equated to approximately 400 pounds, with a street value of just under a quarter of a million dollars.

The packers were all illegal aliens, so they would first face the felonies for the state laws they had broken. Once those sentences were complete, they would be processed through Immigration and returned to their home country.

This was the routine for every one of these groups we apprehended, and they were moving through our county every single night. There was never enough time, resources, or manpower to address all of it. We were under no illusions that we were stopping the flow of drugs smuggled by the cartels through these desert routes, but we were doing our piece and disrupting their flow as best we could.

I've often been asked if I felt it was a losing battle, and I can honestly say I did not. I thought that we were doing what we could, and we were doing a damn good job. In response to that question, I often responded with other questions: "What is the alternative? Do we just forfeit these routes and let them have free reign?"

I, for one, was not open to that option, so we kept fighting and doing our part to fight these battles in our backyard—hoping we could someday win this war.

16.

CARTEL CUP CHECK

AS WE CAME INTO 2012, I was approached by one of our county attorneys. He was very interested in helping us fight our battle against the cartels in our county. We met for coffee one day so he could pick my brain about our operations and maybe identify some of the gaps that his office could potentially help with.

One of his very first questions was, "Matt, what can we do to help you guys?"

Having watched the cartels exploit some of our weak points over and over again and having tried—to no avail—to get federal prosecutors to help us in certain aspects of the smuggling crimes, I was more than ready to answer this. But first, I had to give him a little background on our problems.

I needed to provide him with a breakdown of how we ran our operations and what would and would not get prosecuted. During this particular time, we had fairly good luck prosecuting the drug loads through the federal and state systems, depending on which agency was the lead.

If Homeland Security Investigations (HSI) was the lead agency, and we worked with them, we would generally get cases prosecuted at the federal level. If we were the sole case agents (not working with any other agency), we would prosecute the cases through our county attorneys and the state court.

But when we worked hand-in-hand with Border Patrol, we often had to take over and prosecute their cases through the state court. We did this mainly to pick up the slack when the DEA (Drug Enforcement Agency) would decline to prosecute.

You see, when the cartels were pushing marijuana as the primary commodity through our area, and the Border Patrol intercepted a load with suspects, they were required to contact the on-call DEA agent to have the DEA prosecute the case through federal court. Border Patrol did not have the authority to charge people with these crimes.

The only problem was that the DEA would decline a load of 500 pounds or less. Essentially, the DEA was saying that anything below 500 pounds of marijuana was not worth their time and effort.

So, the Border Patrol then faced a choice. They could confiscate the drugs and let the drug runners be deported and not charged for the additional crime, or they could call us, and we would take the case over and charge the drug runners through our state court.

As luck would have it, the DEA declined quite a few cases, which meant that we got to charge these bad guys through state court. It really helped strengthen our relationship with Border Patrol on joint cases. As we dive deeper into this chapter, you will see that this situation returned even more dividends.

One initial problem we had to tackle with Border Patrol was teaching them the state laws and rules we would use for prosecution. More importantly, we had to teach them about what we would use as reasonable suspicion or probable cause to stop and investigate those we suspected of smuggling.

Another issue we addressed was that our office—

specifically, the sheriff—would have to authorize and sign off on a "cross-certification."

This meant that several Border Patrol agents we worked with on a routine basis would have to go through a short class on some of the vehicle and state laws that applied to our operations. Additionally, the sheriff would have to swear these agents in and deputize them, so they could enforce the laws under the color of the authority of our office.

In layman's terms, it gave the Border Patrol agents the authority to stop for and enforce some limited state laws, and they were now "cross-certified."

This was important because we had to have a solid start on a case to take it over for a successful prosecution. So, having these Border Patrol agents cross-certified meant that there would be a good hand-off from them on the initial contact with the smugglers, and it would allow us to run with the case and prosecute smugglers when the DEA declined the case.

This brings me back to my conversation with the deputy county attorney about how he could help us in our fight. I knew that one of our weak spots in prosecutions was on the cartel scouts and re-supply personnel.

The vicious loop went something like this ... We would apprehend a scout on a hill. When we captured said scout, this person would be a Mexican national one hundred percent of the time. These Mexican nationals would generally dress in camouflage clothing, and we would typically apprehend them close to their assigned location.

If you remember back in Chapter 7, where we described the scouts and their hideouts, you will understand that we would usually catch them with things like binoculars and a radio of some type. Additionally, they would often have phones, solar panels, extra batteries, food, and other camping supplies. These scouts would insist that they were just out hiking and not part of any cartel or smuggling organization.

The same would apply to the re-supply personnel. We would stop a re-supply vehicle, which would be loaded with up to six large, black trash bags. Each bag would be filled with food, batteries, alcohol, cigarettes, radios, phones, camping supplies, clothing, and sometimes weapons and ammo.

Minus the weapons and ammo, the rest of this stuff was not illegal to possess. And even though the occupants of the vehicle had no good explanation as to why they were in the middle of the open Arizona desert in a smuggling corridor, dropping off these bags of supplies, they were not necessarily doing anything against the law.

Understanding what was happening and exactly what these people were involved in did not help us stop them. We would work with Border Patrol to get these bad guys charged through the United States Attorney's Office, but the charges would always get declined. It would be the same for the re-supply guys that we caught.

See, the prosecution of scouts and re-supply personnel as members of the cartels and smuggling organizations takes some work. You must prove that they are part of an organized and orchestrated system. You have to somehow link them to the smuggling activities they are logistically supporting, and the prosecutors did not want to mess with that kind of case.

Prosecutors usually loved using phrases such as "no likelihood of conviction" or "no jury appeal," which often translated to either they did not want to do the work or did not know how to prosecute the case. And they were definitely not about to ask anyone for help.

Explaining all of this to my deputy county attorney, I then replied to his original question by saying that we needed help prosecuting these bastards to affect the logistical branch of the cartels. I explained to him that if we convicted the scouts and the re-supply personnel, this would create a void in the smuggling organizations' operations, giving us an opportunity to exploit that weakness.

I was very passionate about this, as I had seen these people thumb their noses at us and the system while they continued doing their work for the cartels. Luckily, my passion for it lit a fire with my newfound best friend of a prosecutor when he agreed that this was a problem and that it also fired him up. He asked me to give him a couple of days to brainstorm with some of his staff and then promised me that he would help.

True to his word, he asked for another meeting after a few days. We met again, and he laid out some of the historical data that he would need to establish the smuggling activities that had been going on for years in our county. In addition, he would need a few of us to be willing to be qualified as expert witnesses to testify in these cases. Lastly, he told me that I would need to develop a viable plan of attack on a scout interdiction operation, as the scouts were the bad guys he wanted to go after first.

So, I immediately went to work putting together everything he and I discussed in our plan. It was easy to establish expert witnesses. Since we were already working as part of a task force that included both the Border Patrol and Homeland Security Investigations, we had experts in all realms.

Next, we outlined exactly how we would conduct a

scout interdiction operation. This operation would set precedents for both law enforcement and the court system. It would be the first time we formally charged these cartel members for their role as scouts or re-supply personnel. I wanted to make sure that we had our bases covered and used the best people from our side for each aspect of the operation.

I met with Border Patrol and explained our plan for prosecuting the scouts and re-supply personnel. To say that my brothers and sisters in green were excited about the prospect of finally being able to send these people to jail would be an understatement.

I knew from experience that there was one team with the master's degree of getting in on scouts quickly and getting them sacked up to go to jail—and that was the BORTAC team. As I mentioned in the last chapter, this is the Border Patrol's version of a tactical team or SWAT team, and these guys were some squared-away cats.

They had direct access to the air assets we would need to get into the hills, and the agents could be on top of the scouts before they knew what hit them. BORTAC also had the skills necessary to do some high-speed tactical maneuvers out of helicopters to pounce on the scouts before they could shapeshift and disappear.

So, it was only fitting that we asked the BORTAC crew to be the jump-out boys on the operation, which meant that they would be the team that deployed onto the mountaintop sites and apprehended the scouts. (I took a little heat over this decision because some of my team members were also good at this, but I knew that for this operation, it had to be BORTAC.)

Next was the decision on the investigative piece, and for this, it had to be our detectives assigned to our Anti-Smuggling Unit. I met with them, selected the detective who would be the case agent, and discussed how we would structure the case.

The lead detective on a case like this was a big deal because we were breaking new ground here and creating case law based on the prosecution of these cartel members. I selected one of the newer detectives, who was also a member of our SWAT team because I trusted him to follow orders and pay attention to detail—both of these attributes would be key to this operation.

Being the case detective meant that he would handle a lot of the coordination and documentation of the specifics. Careful attention to detail was necessary to ensure that we had an airtight and prosecutable case. He would have to work closely with the prosecuting attorneys, have a well-put-together case file, and have the ability to testify to all of this. It was an enormous ask for a newer detective, but I was confident that he could do it.

Lastly, we decided how we would secure and process the evidence. When you take a scout from a hilltop and out of their mountaintop living quarters and operating area, there is a lot of evidence to document and collect.

Operationally, the BORTAC team that would be inserted for apprehension was just that—the apprehension team. That is really where their responsibility ended. Much like when a SWAT team serves a search warrant on a house, the team's responsibility is to secure the bad guys and the location to make it safe. Then it gets turned over to detectives who collect and pack evidence and interview suspects on-scene.

I knew that Border Patrol had an excellent evidence recovery team. Since they were Border Patrol, it would be easiest to attach them to the BORTAC team responsible for the apprehension. So, that is what I did.

The evidence team would be inserted on the mountaintop with BORTAC. Once the apprehension piece was secure and our bad guys and their hideout were made safe, the Border Patrol evidence team would move in to process and collect the evidence. This evidence team would then meet with our detectives at the bottom of the hill to cleanly hand off the evidence. This would ensure that we had a solid chain of custody of the evidence for the case and prosecution purposes.

With all of these pieces in place, we moved forward with our planning process for the operation itself. This may sound simple, but with air assets, ground assets, and all of the moving parts, it took several months to plan this operation before going live. The prosecution piece also had several moving parts, so we had to ensure that the prosecutors were also included and vested in the overall plan.

The anticipation was palatable as we moved through the planning phase and got closer to going live. We had been waiting a long time to be able to snatch up some scouts, put them in jail, and then send them to prison for their role in furthering the drug cartel operations.

As I have described several times, these scouts were like shapeshifters, and I'm pretty convinced they were also part billy goat. I have seen them disappear in front of me. I have also seen them run like an Olympic sprinter across and down a mountain.

So we would also have a team assigned to move in on the ground by vehicle and get a perimeter set. Of course, the timing on all of this also had to be coordinated so that the ground team did not give away the apprehension team and vice versa.

Scout takedowns would be especially gratifying given some of the scouts' attitudes in recent apprehensions. They basically told us that they would not go to jail. They would be deported and be back in position within days. They had no clue what was about to happen. And we had no clue how successful the operation would be.

The go-day was a cold Arizona winter morning, and rain had moved in. From our perspective, God was on our team because the rain helped to keep the scouts hunkered down in their hideouts and caves on the mountaintops.

But on the flip side, the rain would make the rocky hills very slippery for our guys and would also present some slight problems for the apprehension team's transportation. Additionally, it would make the desert floors a little muddy for the ground teams inserting by vehicle. Nonetheless, the operation was a go, and we were on our way to the early morning briefing.

At the briefing, there was a sense of camaraderie between all of us, despite the different uniforms or patches we wore. That day, we were one team with one mission and one overall goal.

For us, it was finally time to prosecute these bastards

and show everyone that it could be done. For Border Patrol, it was some of the same, with the addition of feeling vindicated for being told by federal prosecutors that it could not be done.

And for everyone involved, it meant that if we were successful, we would put a nice dent in the cartel operations and cause them some issues in their logistics. This translated to slowing them down a little and hopefully exposing some of their internal weaknesses that we could further exploit.

As the briefing was conducted and assignments were made, we heard radio traffic from some of the BORTAC personnel who were already in the mountains watching our locations. We also listened to the confirmation that the BORTAC apprehension teams were spinning up and would be inbound from their off-site location.

This was our cue to finish up and mobilize to head to our target mountain range. As we grabbed our equipment and got into our assigned vehicles, we could feel the overall anticipation that comes before every operation. Things got a little quieter, guys started to focus on their assigned job or task, and everyone started to prepare mentally.

As we headed to the location, there was a little joking, some theme music playing to set the tone, and some lightheartedness before arriving. There was no mistake that we liked to have fun, and we enjoyed our jobs, but we also understood that this job could be deadly. The guys we were about to take down placed no value on human life— especially the life of a cop trying to put them in jail. So, as we got closer to the target and heard the radio chatter from the on-site personnel and apprehension team, things calmed down again, and everyone focused.

We started to see the outlines of the mountaintops as we got closer. The radio chatter stopped after the call of "one minute out" and then "thirty seconds out." This was game time, and we had our game faces on. We dove off the main roadway onto small, two-track desert roads, some of which were nothing more than a trail. Our vehicles raced across the open desert floor, soaked from the overnight rain. As we headed for the base of our target mountains, we could see our aircraft circling the top of the mountains. The BORTAC crew, forward-deployed to observe, called out over the radio that we had good guys on the ground.

Minutes went by that seemed like hours as we waited at the mountain's base for a report. It wasn't long before we started getting sit reps (situational reports) from the apprehension crew …

Over the radio, we heard Apprehension Team One say

they had one in custody. Then we heard Team Two say they had two additional people in custody. We finally got the last report that our third target was GOA (Gone On Arrival). Somehow this scout, who was actually our main target, had slipped away either just before or during the chaos of the insert and takedown.

My team started working our way up the hill to use our binoculars to search the mountainside. Maybe, by some chance, our missing target would make a mistake by moving hiding spots or attempting to outmaneuver one of the Border Patrol agents on the top of the hill. If he did, and we could pinpoint his location from below, it was game-on again.

As we moved to get a better position, we came to a small, concealed cut containing some hidden treasures. These cuts are like miniature canyons between two elevation changes on a hill and can be very hard to see from the bottom. This one was about twenty by thirty yards within the depressed area. In it, we found a cache of car batteries, fuel, some newer-looking backpacks, fresh and full water jugs, and remnants of consumed food.

This cut was a hiding spot for scout supplies that either would not fit in their hilltop hooch or were too visible in that location. This spot would allow them to easily reach their stores without giving away their position or taking up too much space in their campsites.

Once the scene on the top of the mountain settled down and was deemed secured and safe, the Border Patrol evidence team started going to work. Meanwhile, the BORTAC team focused on getting the scouts in custody turned over to our detectives to begin the interview process. We promptly learned that one of the scouts was armed with an AR-15 style rifle, but he offered no resistance, and we recovered the weapon.

The detectives conducted a quick initial interview before taking the three scouts back to our station for a full-on interview. We immediately discovered that two of the gentlemen were simply out hiking and had no idea what was going on. They also claimed that they knew nothing about smuggling or cartels.

Our third guy—the guy with the gun—was a little bolder in his initial statements to our detectives. He said that he was, in fact, a scout who coordinated drug-load movement in these valleys. That was just like a nice little cherry-on-top for us in this case, as his confession solidified our prosecution.

Soon the evidence had been collected from the mountaintops and brought down to be handed off to our detectives. Once they took custody of the evidence and the mountaintop scenes were secured and done, the radio call would go out for everyone to make their way back to the briefing location for the debriefing.

But just before this call went out, radio chatter kicked up about a fire on the hill. Within seconds, we could all see a large plume of smoke near the top of the primary hill. We didn't know what was going on or what was on fire.

This situation quickly amped everyone back up. We then received a report that either a stove or lantern had been knocked over in one of the small scout caves at the top of the hill. The scouts' sleeping bags and some clothing had caught on fire. At that point, the only thing to do was to let it burn itself out, which it did within a few minutes.

With that, the BORTAC teams loaded up and headed back to their base station in Tucson to debrief on their portion of the operation separately. We knew that we would have an overall debrief in the next few days, so the initial debrief was just to address any immediate and pressing concerns about the operation, which would then be discussed later.

All in all, the operation was a success. We had achieved our objective of apprehending the scouts at the locations where they lived and worked, along with any pertinent evidence. We had no injuries to any good guys, and the operation had mostly gone according to plan. Once we met and debriefed, we celebrated a little with congratulations to everyone involved for a successful mission.

My team and I gathered around for a quick picture to memorialize the event because it was one of those historical moments in our careers we would never forget and would be talked about for years to come. We also knew that this was the start of many enforcement actions against scouts and re-supply personnel.

At the time, we did not understand the politics behind what we had just done. In the near future, our operational success on scouts would force federal prosecutors to take another look at prosecuting the scouts at the federal level.

Our detectives wrapped up their interviews with the scouts and transported them to our county jail. The scouts quickly questioned why they were being processed in our jail instead of being taken to the Border Patrol station.

Our detectives explained to them that they were being booked for conspiracy to transport and sell marijuana. Once they finished their prison time for that, they would then be turned over to Border Patrol to be processed for deportation. This was a big surprise to these gentlemen (as we expected it to be), and needless to say, the word spread very quickly through the cartel communication channels about what had happened.

Our prosecutors started working on plea deals with the lawyers for these scouts. The shortest deal was a two-and-a-half-year prison sentence. As these sentences started getting handed down, it became a game-changer for how we dealt with scouts and how they dealt with their jobs.

And before long, federal prosecutors wanted to talk about how they could prosecute these same scouts at the federal level. We had accomplished our mission and got the added bonus of getting them to do their jobs.

This would end up being one of the last, big desert operations I would oversee, as my bosses above me had decided that I needed to run one of our patrol regions. So, I wrapped up my assignment as the commander over SWAT, Narcotics, and Anti-Smuggling and moved to a position overseeing our most-populated and busiest patrol regions.

While I was not in favor of the move, it allowed me some time to slow down and focus on my family a little more. The one thing that always suffers when you spend your time in the smuggling and narcotics world is your family. It becomes a difficult balance to maintain because of the work and hours involved.

As I went into my new assignment, it was bittersweet. But this turned out to be only a short break, as I would return to this same position less than two years later.

17.

CAUSE AND EFFECT

THE MEXICAN CARTELS have had a worldwide impact. They have moved from regional criminal enterprises into transnational criminal organizations, with their hands in everything from gold, to oil, to avocados, to counterfeit goods. Of course, their cash crop has been—and remains to be—the illegal drugs they develop and ship into the United States and around the world.

As we have battled these cartels in Arizona, we have seen firsthand the damage and destruction they cause. As I've said, Arizona is heavily controlled and run by the Sinaloa cartel, which has now fractured after Joaquin "El Chapo" Guzman was captured and imprisoned for the final time.

However, the effects of all the cartels are felt in the United States—especially as they have transformed from groups of smugglers into organized and violent cartels. We in law enforcement watched them morph before our very eyes. They changed from the old-school Mexican gangsters dressed in the traditional Mexican cowboy attire into the modern-day, pretty-boy-type Mafiosos with an almost cult-like following and their own social media pages.

As the transformation began, the older cartel members who were holding onto long-time traditions and a specific set of rules gave way to a younger generation of reckless and violent members who crossed all lines. The older cartel bosses considered business as business, and generally speaking, their families would be left out of it—especially women and children.

In this new era, we have women and children doing the dirty work. There are no boundaries with family when it comes to retribution and the business part of the drug game for these cartels.

The level of violence toward other human beings crossed all previous lines as these cartels grew into today's criminal powerhouses. While old-school cartel members might assassinate a single member from a rival cartel or group violently and publicly, today's cartel members will publicly execute enemies, cut off their heads and genitals, and then hang the bodies from an overpass. This sends a clear warning of fate to enemies who continue to oppose them. This violence is not contained to one area or group, either. The level of violence these cartels use against each other, government officials, and family members of their enemies is seeing rapid and uncontrolled increases because the cartels are acting as if they are in a contest to see who can be the baddest.

Cartel 1 would shoot a Cartel 2 member in public. Then, Cartel 2 would come back and publicly kill a member of Cartel 1 and defame the body. Cartel 1 would respond by capturing a member of Cartel 2 and film that person being interrogated, tortured, and eventually killed. They would release the video on a public forum via the internet.

This vicious cycle would continue, with each group "one-upping" the other until people were being skinned alive. Women's bodies were being mutilated and dumped in a busy public square. Severed heads were even being tossed on dance floors. These cartels had turned into savages, and their members were becoming younger and younger.

As I discussed, the narco culture had become a thing, and these cartel bosses and high-ranking members had their own social media followings. There would be videos of killings and torture constantly shared on these platforms, along with the expensive cars, beautiful women, exotic animals, and piles of money. This display directly influenced the younger generations of up-and-coming narcos as they worked their way into power positions and pushed out the old-school narcos.

The only problem is that we cannot go back. The violence may subside and not be as prolific at times, but the level and means of violence will not return to the good old days. This, in turn, has a very damaging and long-lasting effect on not only the cartels and culture of Mexico but also everyone they deal with.

Again, referring back to the fact that they now operate worldwide means that their influence is much further-reaching than ever before, and their evil roots continue to grow and take hold across the globe.

The cartels used to be just a Mexico movement, but they pushed their way into the U.S. Then, the cartels were just a southwest-border thing, but their tentacles continued to grow and flourish.

These days, every town in the United States with any type of population has a cartel problem. Whether you believe it or not, whether you see it or not, and whether you care about it or not ... They are there.

We in law enforcement know this to be true. You will still find some places throughout the United States that do not yet recognize that they have this problem, but if you live in a community with any drug use or drug issues, there is a cartel connection.

I am not attempting to be an alarmist—I am just being real with you. I watched this scourge expand as the cartels gained more and more power and control of the illegal drug market. These cartels quickly grew like a slow-burning fire with gasoline tossed on it. They have continued like a raging wildfire and have swept across the U.S. and the world, leaving destruction everywhere they touch.

Of course, the cartels are known for their drug smuggling, but they also smuggle people. Declaring that they own and control any and all routes that lead from Mexico into the United States, they rule over all movements in the smuggling corridors. As the cartels smuggle people through these corridors and to their final destination in a stash house somewhere in the Phoenix Metropolitan area, the people are not treated well in the slightest.

The simple truth is this: The Mexican cartels control the illegal immigration through our southern borders. They use illegal immigration to make money from trafficking in people and to take the attention off the metric tons of illicit drugs they are also moving into our country.

If you are an illegal immigrant being transported or guided by the cartel, you are a commodity. That means you are an item. A thing. An object.

You are not viewed as a human being and are treated accordingly. If you become injured along the way, you are left behind because you will only slow the group down. There are no medical stations along the way, and the cartels do not call for help for you. You are simply left in the remote deserts of Arizona, sometimes to die a slow, painful death while you are all alone.

If you are a woman being smuggled by the cartel, you are not only a commodity but also something that the smugglers will use to fulfill their carnal desires. When a cartel member feels the need to satisfy his sexual desires, he does not ask. He simply takes what he wants by force, and many of these women are raped like this multiple times along their journey.

Their bras and panties are taken and draped on trees in the middle of the desert. These trees are called rape trees, and they act as shrines or trophies on display for all to see where women are bound and raped by these evil men.

As a local cop and Arizona native, I have also seen

firsthand everything that goes along with the Mexican cartels that are never talked about or focused on. When the cartels are smuggling drugs, whether by foot or in vehicles, they cause extreme environmental damage to the smuggling corridors they use. The high desert hills and low desert valleys are littered with the infamous and ever-present smuggler trash left behind.

You can walk our beautiful deserts from the border up to our county, and you will find deposits of old clothes, discarded plastic water jugs, food wrappers, abandoned vehicles in areas that are too remote for them to be recovered, and the remnants of drug packs.

These same areas have numerous foot trails and four-wheel-drive roads that were never there before. Many of these appear almost overnight as the cartel changes a route to avoid detection and, in doing so, basically runs down native trees and cactuses to clear the path for travel. If you look at a satellite map of the smuggling corridors and go back in time to previous years, you can see just how much damage these cartels have done to our beautiful Arizona landscape.

All of the evil, hate, and crime in the Mexican cartels are fueled by greed for wealth and power. These are criminals in a criminal syndicate who have their hands in everything, everywhere. They do an outstanding job of controlling their environment while hiding in plain sight.

They feed off our country's demand for drugs, and they love to see the political fights in our country over illegal immigration. While the politicians fight over the broad subject of immigration, this criminal enterprise exploits every piece of the argument to continue its billion-dollar business. And I've already told you about some of the heinous crimes associated with illegal immigration.

I do not know what the solutions to these problems are, but I know that acting like they don't exist and treating the subject with kid gloves will never work.

When we as cops want to dismantle a hardcore criminal organization, we relentlessly chase, disrupt, and imprison them. We confine them and sentence them for hundreds of years while taking all of their assets, including all assets that their families have due to their criminal activity. There is only one way to deal with hardcore criminals: to be hardcore law enforcers who meet them at every turn and continue to lock them up until they are no longer free to do their evil.

You may say it doesn't work, and it can sometimes feel like it is not working. However, we don't get into this job to quit, and we law enforcers have taken down crime boss after crime boss, along with their organizations, through tough and consistent cop work.

There will always be evil because we are humans and are bound to act like it, but there will always be a small percentage of us who are willing to stand up and face that evil. We hang onto these men and women and that hope, knowing that the good guys will always win in the end.

AFTERWORD

AS WE TRAVELED THROUGH all of these time periods, the world was constantly changing. When I started in the dope game, 9/11 had not happened, the Colombians were still the big dogs in the drug world, and the Mexican groups of smugglers had not even become true cartels yet.

As time went on, we moved through all the different phases of the Mexican cartels coming into their own and the Sinaloa cartel becoming the major player in these Transnational Criminal Organizations. I watched as we moved from the social media platform of Myspace into a new world of YouTube, where the cartels would make fun of each other with videos claiming that certain cartel leaders were gay or subservient to others.

Then, we moved into an era of the Boost Mobile phones with their push-to-talk that was so popular with the cartels—and honestly, with us, for that matter. I have to say that push-to-talk was one of the best tools ever for stationary and mobile surveillance.

Along came Facebook and Instagram, and we moved into an era where cartel members and leaders flaunted their riches, women and cars, and exotic animals on these social media platforms.

All during this timeline, one fact remained: the United States was consuming illegal drugs at a record pace. This only served to further fuel the flames for the growth and power of the Mexican cartels.

In the United States, states were moving to legalize marijuana for medicinal and recreational purposes. We also had strict laws taking effect in the United States on precursor chemicals to make methamphetamine.

Then, we had the big pharmaceutical companies making and pushing opiates by the ton to all ages and demographics as the quick fix for whatever ails them. The HMOs also pushed their doctors to no longer care about healing people and instead encouraged the doctors to just mask medical issues with a quick prescription of whatever the best opiate on the market was at that time.

It was a perfect storm for mass drug consumption by the United States, all while our society was going through its natural shifts with each new generation. We were moving fast into new technology. We were moving from dial-up to digital, from cellular phones to handheld computers where everything we needed could be accessed almost instantaneously in the palm of our hand.

As we left the 2000s and moved into the 2010s and beyond, the smuggling landscape changed as rapidly as the rest of the world. The legalization of marijuana in some states began to drive down the demand for Mexican marijuana smuggled in by the cartels. The marijuana grown here in the U.S. was generally of higher quality and potency. Demand was being filled by those now permitted by law to grow marijuana here in the States, both within a state where it was legal and in black-market sales to the states where marijuana was still illegal.

This created a whole new set of problems, including the cartels pushing their way into these U.S. markets rather than continuing to push the metric tons of marijuana from their home country. It was easier and more profitable for the cartels to just muscle in on the legal market and control it from within. The United States was now doing part of their work for them.

All the while, the Mexican cartels still controlled the movement of cocaine into the U.S. In addition, they started growing poppies and turning those poppy fields into heroin to satisfy the newfound love of opiates within our nation. They had also gained control of the methamphetamine market by creating superlabs in Mexico and using the precursor chemicals from their new partners in China. They made the purest and largest quantities of methamphetamine in the world, which they pumped directly into the United States.

The Mexican cartels became the big dogs in the drug world and had a worldwide network. Unfortunately for us, the Sinaloa cartel became the big dogs amongst the Mexican cartels, and they owned the Arizona distribution networks.

We watched the cartels go from trafficking small loads of marijuana, moving two- to three-hundred pounds per load, to moving loads of two- to five-thousand pounds per load. The traditional, small group of backpackers turned into vehicle loads.

They also continued to move cocaine, mostly in hidden compartments in vehicles that would travel through the ports of entry to their stash house destination in the Phoenix Metro area. Once they controlled the methamphetamine production, they heavily used this same method to get their drugs across.

Let's not forget that El Chapo Guzman and the Sinaloa cartel were also the geniuses who exploited the Mexico–United States border through the constant building and use of underground tunnel systems to circumvent crossing over the border. They would just cross under it undetected.

The cartels went from allowing illegal immigrants to cross through the same areas where they ran their drugs to completely restricting anyone from using these routes without prior approval.

They moved from having backpackers carry loads of marijuana to hauling metric tons of marijuana through the desert in vehicles. Then they transitioned to using ultralight planes and ATVs to accomplish the same, moving smaller quantities but more frequently. They eventually went full-circle, back to backpackers hauling the marijuana. As the commodity shifted and heroin and methamphetamines became their cash crops, they used these same routes and methods to get that product into the United States for distribution.

All this took place while the American people's social structure, political climate, and insatiable hunger for drugs continued to evolve. And we have now reached a new point in this battle with the introduction of fentanyl.

The Mexican cartels are extremely talented at knowing what the next "thing" will be for us gabachos in the U.S. Hell, most of the time, that's because they have a clear strategy for determining what the next thing will be.

They saw that Americans have an affinity for pill-popping. They saw soccer moms who couldn't handle the stress of their lives and needed their Xanax escape. They saw the lack of tolerance for any pain and the opiates that go along with that.

The cartels saw that this new fentanyl drug was even more profitable for their organizations. They also figured out that if they focused on manufacturing synthetic drugs such as methamphetamine or fentanyl, they could forego growing and harvesting seasons associated with plant-based drugs. They could also pop up their superlabs, fed by the chemicals from their Chinese connections, and mass-produce illicit, synthetic drugs.

The newest phenomenon is the mass production of what are known as fake oxy pills, or the blue M-30s. The cartels have created their own formula to produce these highly-addictive and highly-toxic pills to mimic the euphoria and pain relief of Oxycodone. They also understand from a marketing perspective that Americans are much more apt to pop a pill than stick a needle in their arms for the same effect.

So, here we are now, in the middle of another crisis, fueled by our desire to escape reality in the first world with the newest drug supplied by the Mexican cartels.

The fight doesn't stop.

Generations of cops before me fought these same problems. The names, faces, and drugs change, but the issues do not. Our society is divided into groups of people who adamantly oppose each other because of their beliefs. But often, their views are dictated by the mainstream media, who no longer have a conscience or any accountability for what they say or do.

All of this only adds to the continued decline of morals, rules, and doing what is right. It focuses on getting whatever you can for yourself and everyone else be damned. I often wonder how close we are to self-destruction.

When asked how I view the United States and the issues we face as a nation, I say that if you read the history of great nations and great empires, we currently look a lot like Rome.

The politicians have a sense of entitlement and somehow believe they are our masters, and we as a people are here to serve them. They operate as if the rules do not apply to them but only to the regular class. They act as a ruling class, honestly believing that they know what is best for us more than we know what is best for ourselves. All the while, they entertain us and throw us small loaves of bread to keep us happy.

How does this correlate to the drug world? Well, with the current state of our nation and those charged with running it, what better way to control your people than to addict them to substances that keep them in an altered reality? Luckily for our nation, we have good men and women willing to stand for what they believe in, stand between good and evil, and hold that thin blue line to keep the good people safe from those who would do them harm.

I raise my glass to these men and women. I dedicate this book to each of you fighting the good fight out there. As a strong American, grounded by my faith and love for my God, I know we will be victorious. I know that I and those like me are willing to sacrifice our lives to make sure of it.

As we finish up, I hope I have provided you with some enlightenment on the battles we have fought and continue to fight to keep our communities safe. Many consider the war on drugs a lost cause, but in my opinion, this is not a war on drugs. This is a war on true evil.

These criminal organizations, now known as Mexican cartels, are evil to their core. As I have outlined for you, they corrupt everything that they touch. While I have many more stories on operations like those discussed in this book, I chose these particular stories to give you the best and broadest view I could, from my perspective, on the fight we faced against the cartels.

My goal was to take you through the last twenty years to show you how the drug war has progressed and how these battles are going on all around you, every single day. I attempted to pull the curtain back to show you what probably most of you were completely unaware of.

Hopefully, this book will act as an eye-opener and stir something in you to not just sit back and remain oblivious but to get involved. Be active in our communities, invest in our youth, and be an agent of change and hope for our future.

Most of all, I want you to understand how much the men and women who put on a uniform and leave their families each day care about their communities and fight the evil constantly banging at the doors.

Thank you for reading my book. God bless each of you, and may God continue to bless this great nation.

ACKNOWLEDGMENTS

IT TAKES A LOT TO WRITE A BOOK and even more to prepare it for—and actually publish—said book. Venturing into this new territory, I really had no idea all of the research and work that would go into this.

The thing that absolutely saved me and helped me complete this project was the great network of family and friends that I have. This network, combined with my drive to acknowledge and record the great work that our law enforcement did, was the driving factor pushing me forward on this project.

Before I get into that, I want to recognize a few very special people in my life. First off, as a man of renewed faith, I want to thank God for the blessings in my life. One of those blessings is my wife, who has been my absolute rock through my crazy career and has always been my biggest supporter.

Second, my mom, who has always believed in me, pushed me, and raised me to be the man I am. My Uncle Jim, Aunt Kathy, and Uncle David, who taught me a lot about hunting and the outdoors, which helped me when I moved into the career of hunting evil men.

Lastly, my Grandma and Grandpa, who lived through the great depression, fought in WWII, set a great example for me as a kid, and taught me a lot about people and life.

There are some special people I spent many nights with, away from our families, doing great work against these bad guys.

To honor just a few of you, I want to give a special thanks and shout-out to Tino, Fabio, Tubby, The CJL, the whole old-school SAR crew, my brothers and sisters from the Border Patrol (especially the CAG and AJO stations), my brothers and sisters from the T.O. and G.R. reservations, the West Desert Task Force, the BORTAC crew from Del Rio (Texas), our HSI and ICE peeps, and my Arizona Highway Patrol family.

Last but not least, our counterparts from the HIDTA Task Force, run by the Maricopa County Sheriff's Office (a.k.a. the Vekol Valley Stingers). They always had our backs and helped us step up our game.

As for the people who helped me move this book from

a joking suggestion to the fruition of a finished product, I wanted to give a very humble and sincere thank you.

I want to start with my good friend Katie Pavlich. Katie has guided me through this whole crazy process and encouraged me along the way. I could not have done this without her guidance and help.

Also, my boss, the American Sheriff, Mark Lamb, for actually pushing me to get this done, talking me off the ledge at times, and giving me great insight.

A few more who helped me along the way, whether through direct help, advice, encouragement, or insight, were Biss, Randy S., Leslie P., Ben T., Jason S., Dr. Jason, Ed T., and my man Joey, a.k.a. Warpaint, for the awesome artwork that became part of the book promotional material. Joe V. for the phenomenal job on the book cover. Then there was the editing team: Lori Lynn and Kathy Haskins put as much heart and soul into editing this book as I did writing it. Many more gave advice, input, and help along the way. So, thank you to any I have missed.

Also, a huge thank you to all the men and women who I have worked alongside in this crazy career. It has truly been my honor. I am blessed to have a network of family, friends, and professional contacts to lean on when I need them.

Lastly, I want to thank the men and women who continue to hold that thin blue line across the world. You matter more than you know, and you are appreciated more than you know. Keep the faith, keep your head up, and keep pushing forward.

GLOSSARY OF TERMS

The terms listed below are defined by the author according to his training and experience. The definition given is the definition as it has been used in the area(s) that he lived and worked. Some definitions may have multiple meanings.

Backpackers or Packers – Individuals who enter the United States from Mexico and walk through the open desert carrying illegal drugs to a predetermined location.

Barrio – The literal translation is a district or a town, but as used in the United States, it refers to a neighborhood. Usually used by Mexican culture in the context of which gang controls that particular area.

BORTAC – Border Patrol's version of a tactical team or SWAT team. This team is highly-trained and operates much like a special forces team under the Border Patrol command.

Caballero – The literal translation is a gentleman, but when used as slang, it refers to a cowboy.

Carpet Booties – Special shoe coverings, usually made of cloth and carpet. These fit over a shoe, and the carpet covers the sole of the shoe. Smugglers and packers use them to hide their shoe prints when they are walking through the dirt/desert.

Cartel – Most commonly refers to an organized regional crime syndicate in Mexico. Usually, a cartel operates from, or in, a specific region of the country.

Corridos or Narcocorridos – Songs or folk songs that usually have lyrics referring to the criminal activity of the cartels, mainly focused on the drug trade. Many times, certain cartel bosses or cartels are glorified within these songs.

Corridors – Specific geographic areas controlled and used by the Mexican cartels. Very similar to "plazas" in that these corridors are considered owned and operated by the cartel in control of that area.

Coyote – Slang term referring to a person who guides undocumented aliens from Mexico into the United States.

Cuerno de Chivo – Literal translation is "horn of the goat," but also a slang term that refers to an AK-47 rifle.

Dope – Slang term referring to illegal drugs, and in southern Arizona, usually referring specifically to marijuana.

Driver – An individual operating any type of vehicle as their main job for the cartel. These vehicles carry people, drugs, money, weapons, or supplies.

DTO – Acronym meaning Drug Trafficking Organization

Flashbang – Slang name for a Noise-Flash Diversionary Device, which is a small device that can look similar to a small grenade and is used by SWAT teams and special forces teams to disorient suspects or combatants

Gabacho – The literal translation is "French." However, the word is used to describe people or things from the United States. It is synonymous with gringo.

Gringo – Used by Mexicans to describe something or someone from the United States. Sometimes used in a derogatory manner.

Guero – A term used in Mexico to describe anyone with fair hair and fair/light skin.

Heat Vehicle - Refers to any vehicle used by smugglers to either draw attention away from an actual load vehicle or to interfere with the apprehension of a load vehicle by law enforcement. These vehicles will also be used to drive certain roads or routes to ensure that there is no law enforcement presence.

Interdiction - In law enforcement, this work involves intercepting illegal drugs, currency, people, or other illegal commodities.

Jesus Malverde – Known as the patron saint of drug traffickers. A "Robin Hood" type figure who is believed to have been killed in the early 1900s in Sinaloa. He appears as a Hispanic male with dark hair, a thick mustache, and a white shirt. He has a very loyal following of those involved in cartels and drugs. They pray and make offerings to him in return for safe passage of their drugs or successful operations of their illegal business. Commonly found as statues.

"La Frontera" or Line – Refers to the international border of the United States and Mexico, with the south side of the line referring to Mexico and the north side of the line referring to the U.S.

Load Vehicle - Any vehicle designed to carry or is actually carrying illicit contraband, or is used for human trafficking.

LP/OP – Acronym meaning Listening Post/Observation Post, which is an area used to listen, observe, and report any pertinent activity that the LP/OP overlooks. Both law enforcement and the drug cartels used LP/OPs.

Mafioso – A member of the mafia, but in street slang, can refer to cartel bosses or connected members in the cartel.

Narc – A common street-slang term referring to an undercover police officer who works against illegal drugs.

Narcoculture – The culture specific to the Mexican cartels, which is actually a combination of Mexican culture and the sub-culture created by the cartels and the criminal syndicates associated with them. This includes things such as music, dress, and religious beliefs.

Plaza – The area or territory cartels use to conduct business. A plaza is generally associated with a geographical area and can be as simple as a certain town or as complex as an entire region covering several cities or states. Plazas are considered the sole operating area of a particular cartel or branch of a cartel. When the Mexican cartels were originally split into regions/plazas, there were five, and they were defined by where that specific group operated from and through. The easiest way to think of plazas is like traditional street gangs' areas of control.

Re-Supply – Providing the necessary logistical supplies, usually for scouts, and typically utilizing a vehicle. These supplies can consist of things such as water, food, alcohol, batteries, weapons, ammunition, and cooking supplies.

Rip Crew – A group of individuals (two or more) who forcefully rob people transporting illegal drugs or undocumented aliens. These crews generally operate in more remote areas and use violence to accomplish their robbery.

Santa Muerte – A figure most commonly referred to as a female and looks like a combination of the grim reaper and Holy Mary (Mother of Jesus). Thought to have derived from Saint Death and has a cult-like following who believe that praying to and making offerings to her will ensure those wishes come to fruition. Most commonly found as statues, jewelry, and on religious sites like candles, jewelry, and clothing. Often found in conjunction with pictures of AK-47s and the marijuana leaf.

Scout – An individual working for the cartel and acting as a lookout. In this writing, these individuals usually operate in key locations where they can overlook a specific area for the cartel and report via phone or radio any activity in that area.

Sicario – Spanish word used for a hired gunman, hired killer, or assassin.

Smugglers – Most commonly used to refer to those individuals or groups of individuals who carry or transport illegal drugs or undocumented aliens into the United States from Mexico.

Smuggler Trash – Trash such as discarded clothing, burlap sacks, backpacks, and food wrappers left behind in the open desert by smugglers, packers, or undocumented aliens.

Soldado – Spanish word meaning "soldier." As it relates to cartels and gangs, a soldado refers to lower-level members who carry out orders of the bosses, i.e., assaults, killings, and drug business.

SWAT – Acronym for Special Weapons And Tactics, a police/sheriff team specially-trained to handle high-risk or extraordinary calls.

TCO – Acronym meaning Transnational Criminal Organization. As defined by the FBI: Those self-perpetuating associations of individuals who operate transnationally for the purpose of obtaining power, influence, and monetary and/or commercial gains, wholly or in part by illegal means, while protecting their activities through a pattern of corruption and/or violence, or while protecting their illegal activities through a transnational organizational structure and the exploitation of transnational commerce or communication mechanisms.

TOC – Acronym meaning "Tactical Operation Center," which is usually a motorhome-type vehicle with radios, computers, and other equipment, used as a mobile station/office. Similar to a mobile command post.

MATT IS A NATIVE OF ARIZONA, growing up in Phoenix. He is married to his wife Susie of 29 years and has three children.

Matt has been employed with the Pinal County Sheriff's Office for over 29 years, starting his career as a Detention Officer in 1993 and promoted through the ranks to his current position of Chief Deputy. He has served in several specialty units—Detention, Patrol, Traffic, Training, the Police Academy, Motors, Narcotics, and Investigations.

Having served 18 years on the Pinal Regional SWAT

team as a member, team leader, and finishing as the team commander, he was involved in and/or led over 700 missions during his tenure on SWAT.

Matt has also worked in an undercover capacity, both as a detective and as a sergeant, while assigned to the Narcotics Unit. He has worked and supervised everything from street-level drug cases to large, organized-crime cases in a cartel-infested environment.

Matt's current assignment is as the Sheriff's Executive Officer, serving as second-in-command for the agency. He oversees and manages all operations for over 650 employees and volunteers in a county that covers over 5,400 square miles and has an approximate population of 500,000.

He has served as a regional representative and the Vice President of the Arizona Tactical Officers Association and is a member of the Executive Board for the Point 27 Foundation. He is a graduate of Leadership in Police Organizations and the FBI National Academy, session 261.

Matt holds additional duties as a law enforcement trainer for basic and advanced officer training in leadership, tactics, narcotics, Mexican cartels, and several other specialty areas. He has instructed for High Intensity Drug

Trafficking Areas (HIDTA), National Tactical Officers Association, Arizona Narcotics Investigators Association, Washington State Investigators Association, Georgia FBI National Academy State Chapter, National Rifle Association, and multiple agencies throughout the U.S.

Matt serves as an expert on the Southwest border issues and the problems associated with the Mexican cartels in Arizona. He has spearheaded large-scale operations targeting the Mexican cartels and smuggling operations at the local, state, and federal levels.

Matt is known for his collaborative efforts in working with local, state, and federal partners to fight organized crime in his county, state, and nation. He continues to do his part in fighting these criminal groups.

CONNECT WITH THE AUTHOR

 @DEPUTY_ONETIME

/DEPUTY_ONETIME

DEPUTYONETIME@GMAIL.COM

CPSIA information can be obtained
at www.ICGtesting.com
Printed in the USA
LVHW020547161122
733267LV00013B/599